MODERN BAND SONGBOOK

Bass

Book 1

Skye Claire Hale
Mary Claxton
Scott Burstein

Contributors:

Dave Wish, Tony Sauza, Clayton McIntyre, Lauren Brown, Joe Panganiban

ISBN 979-8-3501-1002-9

Visit Hal Leonard Online at
www.halleonard.com

World headquarters, contact:
Hal Leonard
7777 West Bluemound Road
Milwaukee, WI 53213
Email: info@halleonard.com

In Europe, contact:
Hal Leonard Europe Limited
Dettingen Way
Bury St Edmunds, Suffolk, IP33 3YB
Email: info@halleonardeurope.com

In Australia, contact:
Hal Leonard Australia Pty. Ltd.
4 Lentara Court
Cheltenham, Victoria, 3192 Australia
Email: info@halleonard.com.au

Contents

Introduction

Hello and welcome to the supplemental Songbook for the Modern Band Method (MBM) book series! This book is designed to expand upon the ten Full Band Songs in the MBM series with additional notated repertoire selections, enabling you to play a wider variety of songs. It can also be used as a supplement to other beginner instrument methods.

How to Use This Book

The songs are aligned with the lesson progression of the *Modern Band Bass Method*, incorporating the same skills acquired in each section and consistently building on them.

This book will utilize the same iconic music notation from the MBM series and the parallel tablature and standard notation (where applicable). If any new musical skills are introduced in the selections of this book that are not covered in the MBM series, they will be noted.

Bass Solos

Notes and scales for bass grooves and solos accompany each song chart in the book. Bassists rarely take solos in modern band settings, but we've included these notes to guide you in improvisation and composition. Whether you want to play a melodic solo or compose a new groove, the notes provided will be a good starting point.

Song Arrangements

Some of the songs in this book are presented in different keys than the original recordings. This information is listed at the start of each song. When listening to these songs and trying to play along, the parts you play won't sound correct if you're in a different key than the recording. However, you're still encouraged to listen to the original recordings to gain a better understanding of each song's style, rhythm, and other musical elements.

JUST THE WAY YOU ARE

Bruno Mars

Key of Recording: F
Key of Notation: G
Form of Recording: Intro–Verse 1–Chorus–Verse 2–Chorus–Bridge–Chorus
(For Use with Section 1 of the *Modern Band Bass Method*)

Song Tips:

- Like the chord progression of "I Gotta Feeling" from the Modern Band Method, "Just the Way You Are" is a repeated 8-bar loop. Once you have learned that, you can perform the entire song.
- Refer to the bass note diagrams below for the notes G, E, and C. Instead of finding these different notes on different strings, you could also choose to play G, C, and E all on the E string: C on the 8th fret, G on the 3rd, and E using the open string.
- You can play a variety of comping patterns (rhythms) in different sections of the song, such as playing whole notes in the verse and eighth notes in the chorus.

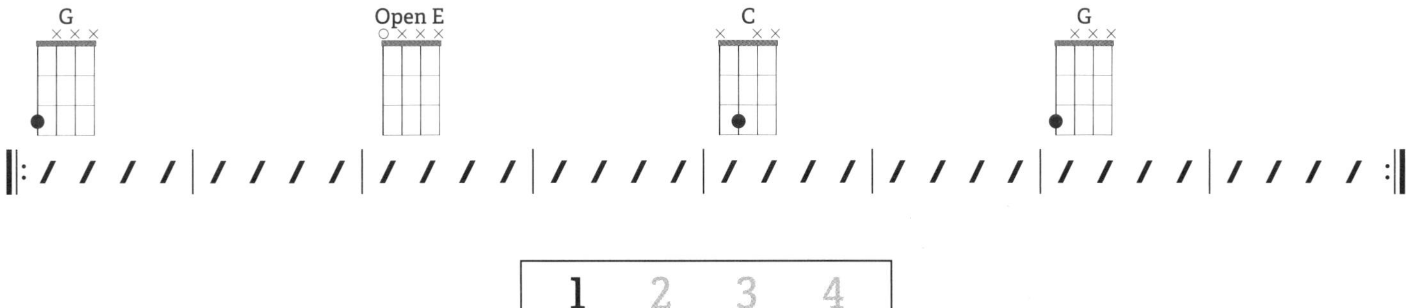

Two-Note Groove (G):

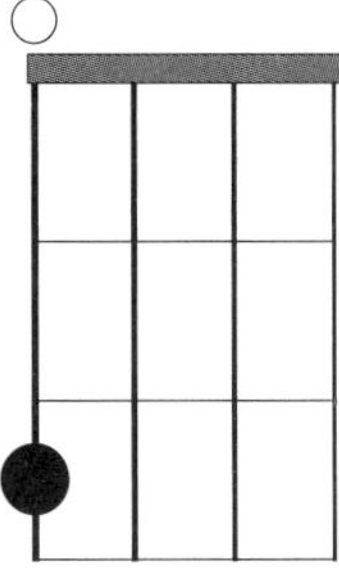

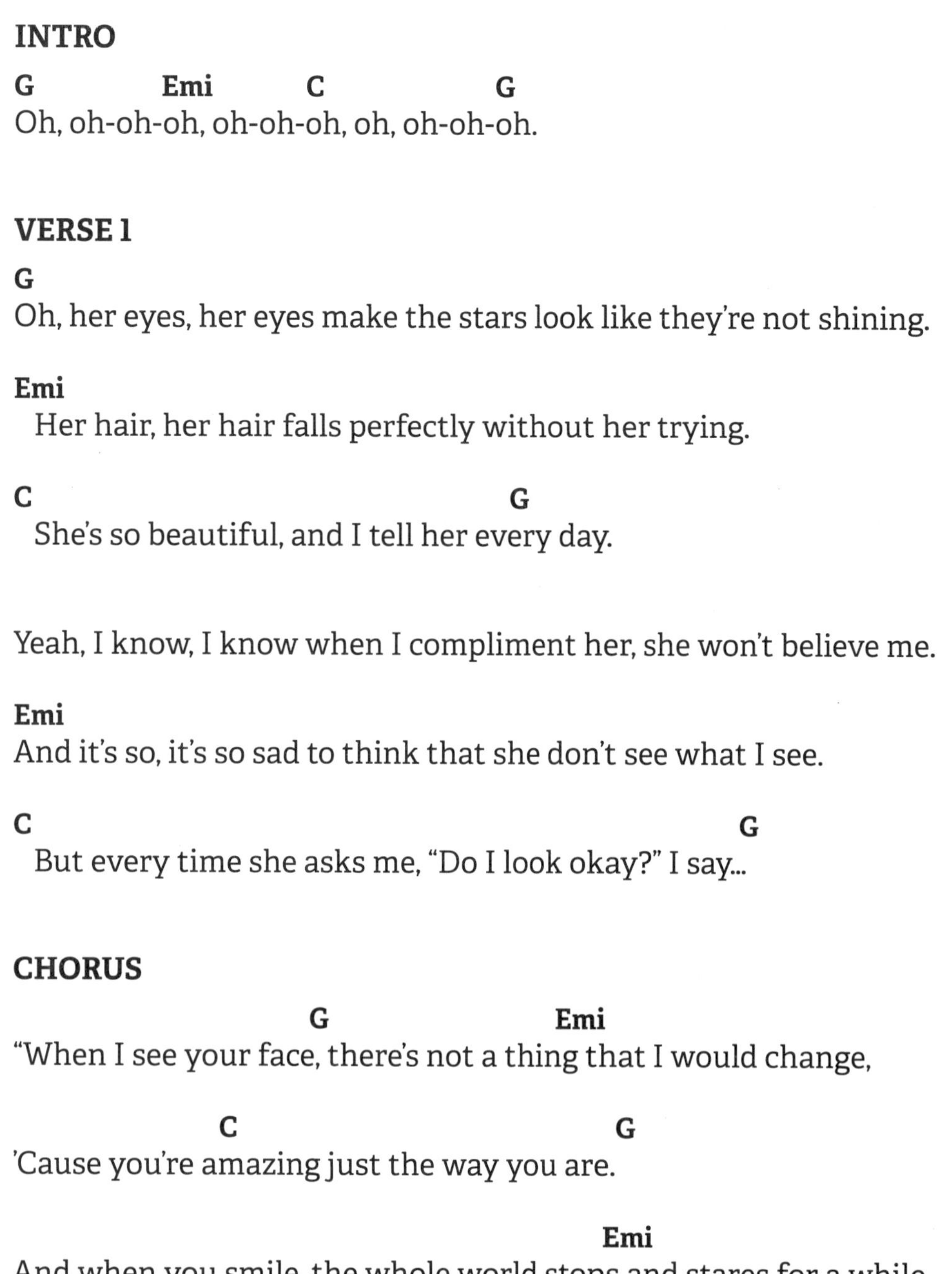

INTRO

G   Emi   C   G
Oh, oh-oh-oh, oh-oh-oh, oh, oh-oh-oh.

VERSE 1

G
Oh, her eyes, her eyes make the stars look like they're not shining.

Emi
Her hair, her hair falls perfectly without her trying.

C   G
She's so beautiful, and I tell her every day.

Yeah, I know, I know when I compliment her, she won't believe me.

Emi
And it's so, it's so sad to think that she don't see what I see.

C   G
But every time she asks me, "Do I look okay?" I say...

CHORUS

G   Emi
"When I see your face, there's not a thing that I would change,

C   G
'Cause you're amazing just the way you are.

Emi
And when you smile, the whole world stops and stares for a while,

C   G
'Cause girl, you're amazing just the way you are."

VERSE 2

G
Her lips, her lips, I could kiss them all day if she'd let me.

Emi
Her laugh, her laugh, she hates, but I think it's so sexy.

C   G
She's so beautiful, and I tell her every day.

Oh, you know, you know, you know I'd never ask you to change.

Emi
If perfect's what you're searching for, then just stay the same.

C   G
So, don't even bother asking if you look okay, you know I'll say...

REPEAT CHORUS

BRIDGE

G   Emi
The way you are, the way you are,

C   G
Girl, you're amazing just the way you are.

REPEAT CHORUS

WHAT ABOUT US

P!nk

Key of Recording: A♭
Key of Notation: G
Form of Recording: Intro–Verse 1–Chorus–Verse 2–Chorus–Interlude–Bridge–Chorus
(For Use with Section 1 of the *Modern Band Bass Method*)

Song Tips:

- "What About Us" is a great foundational song for beginning bass players because it repeats the first three notes you've learned in the same pattern throughout. Take this opportunity to focus on the basics of bass playing. Keep your mind and body relaxed. Pay close attention to the sound of each note you produce—the initial attack of the note with the pick or finger, the duration (length or sustain) of the note, and the end of the note. Does it all sound good to you? If any part doesn't sound right, examine your technique more closely and adjust until it sounds better.
- In the final chorus of the song, you can build intensity in the music by playing the notes on each beat of the measure instead of only on beat 1.

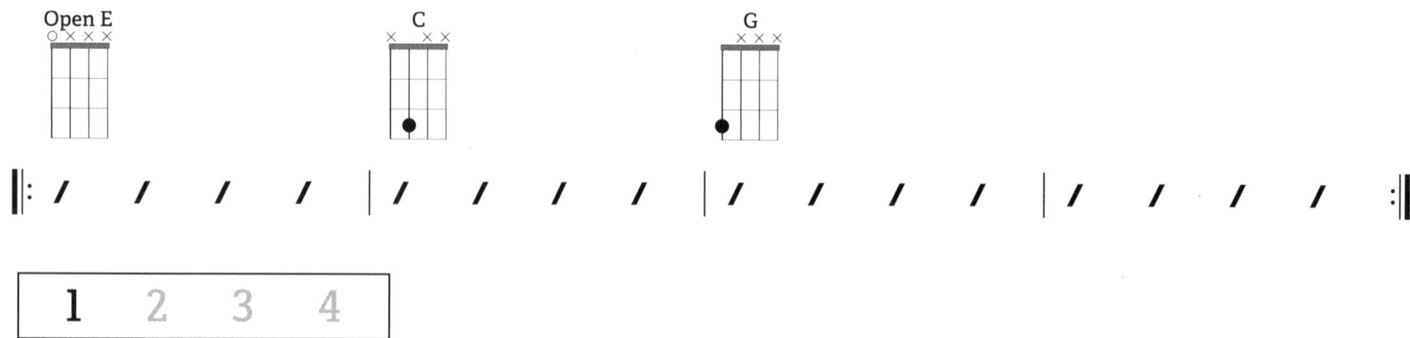

1 2 3 4

Two-Note Groove (G):

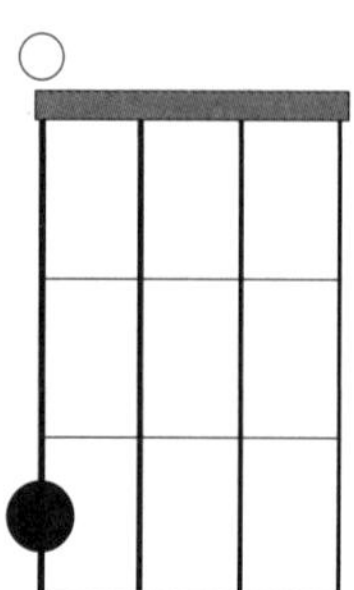

INTRO

Emi   C   G
La-da-da-da-da, la-da-da-da-da. Da-da-da.

VERSE 1

        Emi   C   G
We are search lights; we can see in the dark.

       Emi   C   G
We are rockets pointed up at the stars.

       Emi   C   G
We are billions of beautiful hearts.

         Emi   C   G
And you sold us down the river too far.

CHORUS

            Emi   C   G
What about us? What about all the times you said you had the answers?

            Emi   C   G
What about us? What about all the broken happy-ever-afters?

            Emi   C   G
What about us? What about all the plans that ended in disaster?

            Emi   C   G
What about love? What about trust? What about us?

VERSE 2

        Emi   C   G
We are problems that want to be solved.

        Emi   C   G
We are children that need to be loved.

         Emi   C   G
We were willing, we came when you called.

              Emi   C   G
But man, you fooled us; enough is enough.

REPEAT CHORUS

INTERLUDE

```
             Emi              C                               G
What about us? What about all the plans that ended in disaster?

             Emi                C                 G
What about love? What about trust? What about us?
```

BRIDGE

```
Emi                              C                             G
Sticks and stones, they may break these bones, but then, I'll be ready. Are you ready?

Emi                 C                     G
It's the start of us waking up, come on. Are you ready? I'll be ready.

Emi                   C                 G
I don't want control; I want to let go. Are you ready? I'll be ready.

       Emi              C              G
'Cause now it's time to let them know we are ready. What about us?
```

REPEAT CHORUS

HALO

Beyoncé

Key of Recording: A
Key of Notation: G
Form of Recording: Intro–Verse 1–Pre-Chorus–Chorus–Verse 2–Pre-Chorus–Chorus–Interlude–Pre-Chorus–Chorus
(For Use with Section 2 of the *Modern Band Bass Method*)

Song Tips:

- Though the chord progression in "Halo" doesn't ever change, the instruments and sounds playing those chords change regularly. Some of the original parts, like the opening piano, are quite complex. Others, like the synth whole notes, are much simpler rhythmically.
- You may want to play a simpler or more complex comping pattern depending on how you interpret the song and want to perform it. Your comping pattern may change throughout the performance as well, for example, by playing just on beat 1 during the verse, and then switching to playing on every beat during the chorus.
- The bass part of this song is crucial for establishing the foundation and enriching the overall sound. However, this part should remain relatively simple to allow space for the vocalist. A great bass line is often just a straightforward part that enhances the fullness and impact of everything else. If you want to vary your part, you could play whole notes during the more open sections of the song and switch to quarter or eighth notes in the larger, more driving segments of the song.

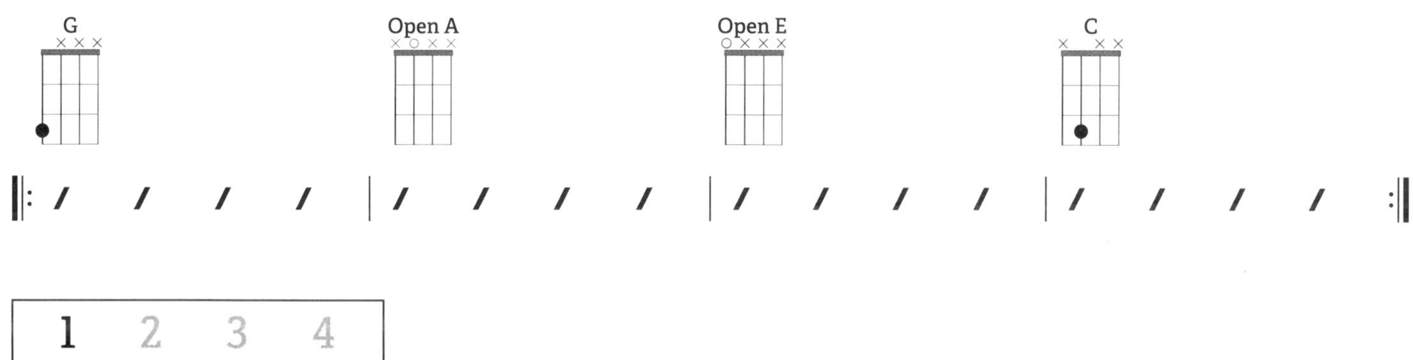

Four-Note Groove (G):

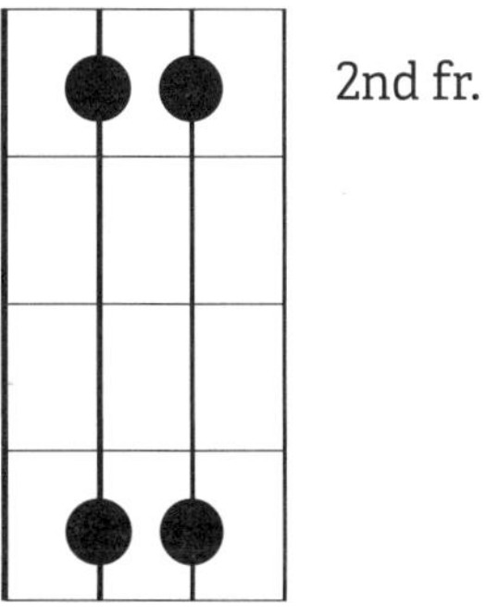

VERSE 1

G **Ami** **Emi**
Remember those walls I built? Well, baby, they're tumblin' down.

C **G**
And they didn't even put up a fight; they didn't even make a sound.

Ami **Emi**
I found a way to let you in, but I never really had a doubt.

C **G**
Standin' in the light of your halo, I got my angel now.

Ami **Emi**
It's like I've been awakened. Every rule I had you breakin'.

C
It's the risk that I'm takin'. I ain't never gonna shut you out.

PRE-CHORUS

G **Ami** **Emi**
Everywhere I'm lookin' now, I'm surrounded by your embrace.

C **G**
Baby, I can see your halo. You know you're my savin' grace.

Ami **Emi**
You're everything I need and more. It's written all over your face.

C **G**
Baby, I can feel your halo. Pray it won't fade away.

CHORUS

G **Ami**
I can feel your halo, halo, halo. I can see your halo, halo, halo.

Emi **C**
I can feel your halo, halo, halo. I can see your halo, halo, halo.

VERSE 2

G   Ami   Emi
  Hit me like a ray of sun, burnin' through my darkest night.

                                    C   G
You're the only one that I want, think I'm addicted to your light.

                             Ami   Emi
I swore I'd never fall again, but this don't even feel like fallin'.

                     C   G
Gravity can't begin to pull me back to the ground again.

                                      Ami   Emi
Feels like I've been awakened. Every rule I had you breakin'.

                             C
The risk that I'm takin'. I'm never gonna shut you out.

REPEAT PRE-CHORUS

REPEAT CHORUS (2 TIMES)

INTERLUDE

G   Ami   Emi   C
Ooh.   Halo.   Halo.

G   Ami   Emi   C
  Ooh.

REPEAT PRE-CHORUS

REPEAT CHORUS (2 TIMES)

SAVE YOUR TEARS

The Weeknd

Key of Recording: C
Key of Notation: C
Form of Recording: Intro–Verse 1–Pre-Chorus–Verse 2–Pre-Chorus–Bridge 1–Chorus–Verse 3–Pre-Chorus–Bridge 2–Chorus–Pre-Chorus–Chorus
(For Use with Section 2 of the *Modern Band Bass Method*)

Song Tips:

- Perhaps the biggest challenge facing bass players in performing this song is consistency. Even though the part contains only eighth notes on the roots, playing those notes with consistent timing and duration for an entire four-minute song is no small feat. If you are playing with a pick, try using only down picks to help maintain consistent *articulation* (how a note is attacked, how long it lasts, and how it connects to other notes). Then, as an extra challenge, try *alternate picking* (alternating downstrokes and upstrokes) with the goal of achieving that same consistent sound. If you're plucking with your fingers, you could try using just one finger to produce a consistent sound, and then attempt to recreate that sound using two alternating fingers.
- While "Save Your Tears" has a fairly consistent rhythm and chords, there are a few breaks. A "break" is when the groove of the song changes and several instruments stop playing. The chorus of the song is a perfect example of this. Much of the accompaniment drops out as the Weeknd sings "Save your tears for another day." Then the whole band comes back in before dropping out once again for the repeated line. As you create your own arrangement with your bandmates, try coming up with a creative way to make this section stand out.
- **Optional Bridge:** This song contains two short bridge sections with some notes you might not know yet. Try out D and F using the note diagrams shown here and add the bridge to your song performance.

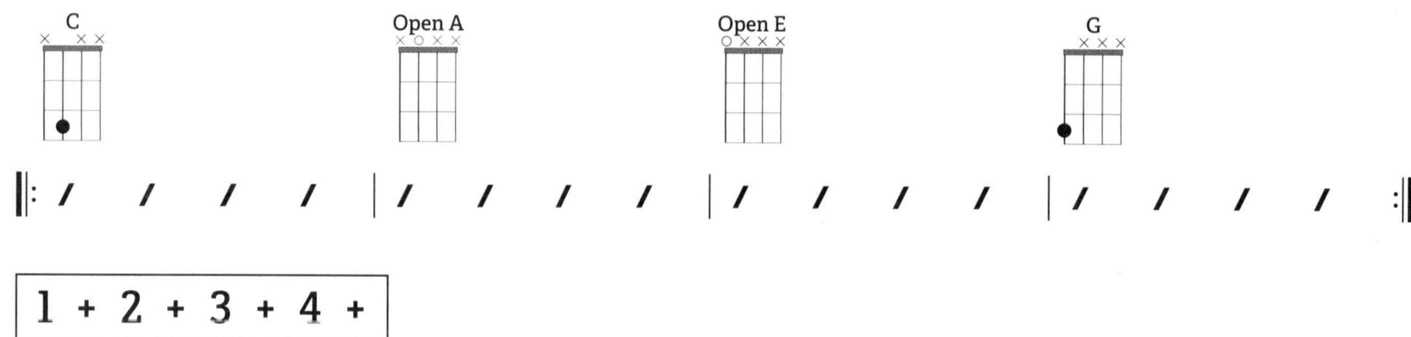

Optional Bridge:

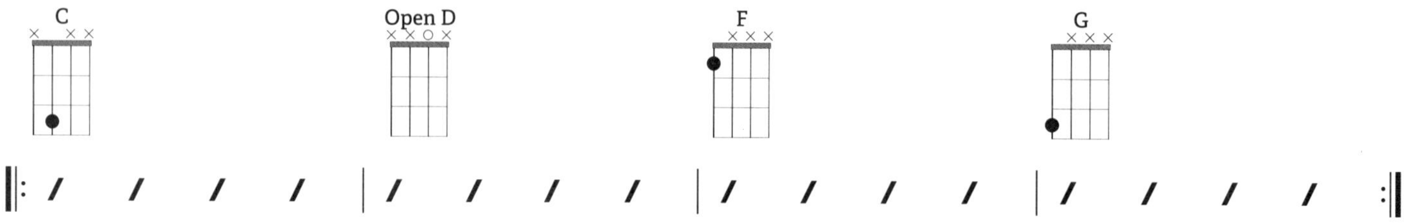

Four-Note Groove (C):

VERSE 1

C **Ami** **Emi** **G**
I saw you dancing in a crowded room. You look so happy when I'm not with you.

C **Ami** **Emi** **G**
But then you saw me, caught you by surprise; a single teardrop falling from your eye.

PRE-CHORUS

C **Ami** **Emi** **G**
I don't know why I run away.

C **Ami** **Emi** **G**
I'll make you cry when I run away.

VERSE 2

C **Ami** **Emi** **G**
You could've asked me why I broke your heart. You could've told me that you fell apart.

C **Ami** **Emi** **G**
But you walked past me like I wasn't there, and just pretended like you didn't care.

REPEAT PRE-CHORUS

BRIDGE 1

Dmi **Ami** **F** **G**
Take me back 'cause I wanna stay. Save your tears for another...

CHORUS

C Ami Emi G
Save your tears for another day.

C Ami Emi G
Save your tears for another day.

VERSE 3

C Ami Emi G
I made you think that I would always stay. I said some things that I should never say.

C Ami Emi G
Yeah, I broke your heart like someone did to mine, and now you won't love me for a second time.

REPEAT PRE-CHORUS

BRIDGE 2

Dmi Ami F
Girl, take me back 'cause I wanna stay. Save your tears for another...

Dmi Ami F G
I realize that I'm much too late and you deserve someone better.

REPEAT CHORUS

REPEAT PRE-CHORUS

REPEAT CHORUS (2 TIMES)

Words and Music by Abel Tesfaye, Max Martin, Jason Quenneville, Oscar Holter and Ahmad Balshe

DREAMS

Fleetwood Mac

Key of Recording: A Minor
Key of Notation: E Minor
Form of Recording: Intro–Verse 1–Pre-Chorus–Chorus–Interlude–Verse 2–Pre-Chorus–Chorus
(For Use with Section 3 of the *Modern Band Bass Method*)

Song Tips:

- The bass focuses on the same groove throughout the song. You can play just whole notes if you want a simpler part. If that's too simple, try slightly modifying the rhythm and/or adding some notes from the six-note groove.
- This song features an interlude section after the first chorus where the chord pattern changes. You can play the same comping pattern as before, or you could experiment with varied or improvised rhythms in this part of the song, as heard in the original recording.

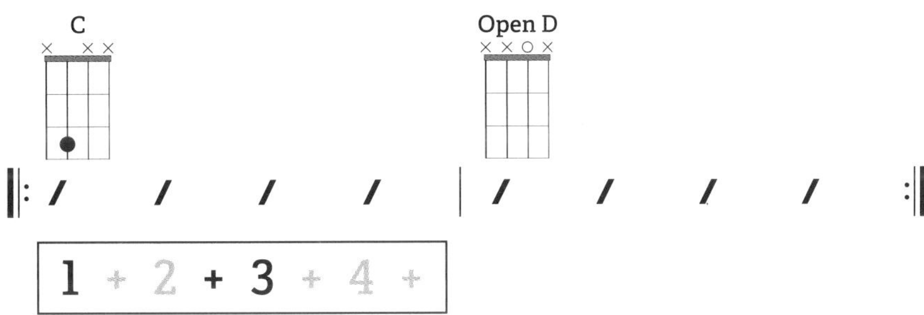

Interlude:

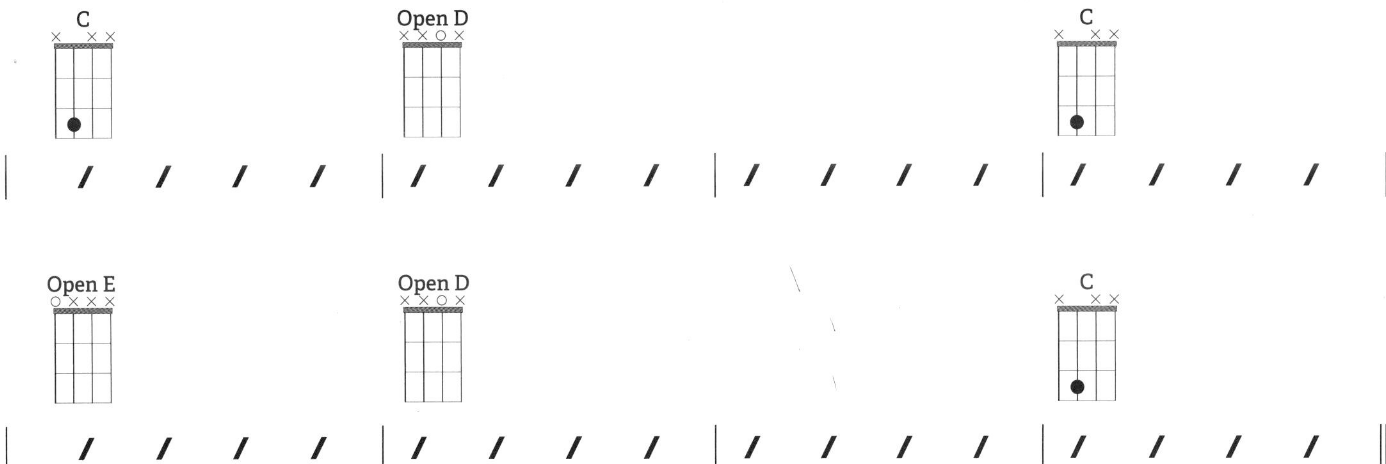

Six-Note Groove (E Minor):

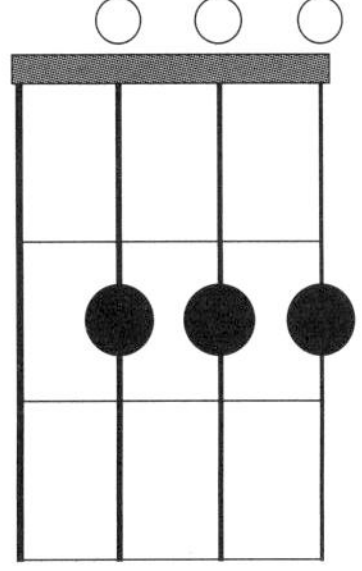

VERSE 1

```
C                D             C                 D
 Now here you go again, you say you want your freedom.

C              D                  C    D
 Well, who am I to keep you down?

C             D                C                D
 It's only right that you should play the way you feel it.

     C           D            C            D
But listen carefully to the sound of your loneliness,
```

PRE-CHORUS

```
       C                   D
Like a heartbeat, drives you mad

          C         D
In the stillness of remembering

              C         D
What you had

                   C    D
And what you lost.

                   C    D
And what you had

                   C    D
And what you lost.
```

CHORUS

```
     C              D                C     D
Oh, thunder only happens when it's raining.

C              D                     C     D
Players only love you when they're playing.

     C                 D                  C    D
Say women, they will come and they will go.

C                    D               C    D
When the rain washes you clean, you'll know. You'll
```

INTERLUDE

```
C      D           C
Know.

Emi    D           C
```

VERSE 2

```
C            D          C            D
  Now, here I go again, I see the crystal vision.

C            D        C      D
  I keep my visions to myself.

C          D            C                  D
  It's only me who wants to wrap around your dreams and,

C              D                C            D
Have you any dreams you'd like to sell? Dreams of loneliness,
```

REPEAT PRE-CHORUS

REPEAT CHORUS (2 TIMES)

SUNFLOWER

Post Malone and Swae Lee

Key of Recording: D
Key of Notation: D
Form of Recording: Intro–Verse 1–Chorus–Verse 2–Bridge–Chorus–Outro
(For Use with Section 4 of the *Modern Band Bass Method*)

Song Tips:

- During parts of the song, the main groove drops out, creating more space for the vocals. You and your band might choose to recreate the changes as they are done in the recording, or you can develop your own rendition. Listen closely for the various changes, their emotional impact, and think about how you might want to replicate those technical and/or emotional shifts.
- The bass part in the original recording is actually a synthesizer. Many bass players also learn to play bass lines on the keyboard. You may want to learn these notes on the keyboard or collaborate with a keyboard player to find a pattern that blends well together.

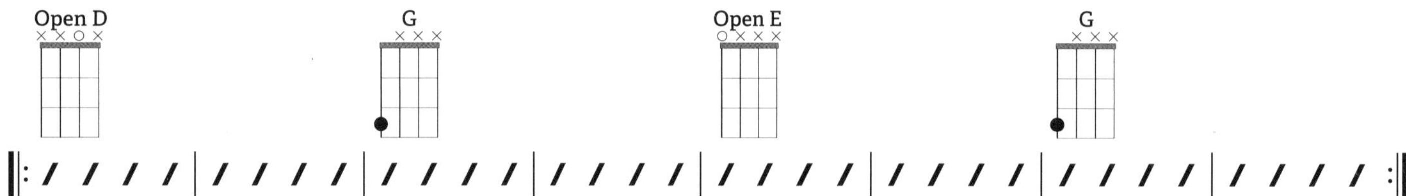

1 + 2 + 3 + 4 +

Six-Note Groove (D):

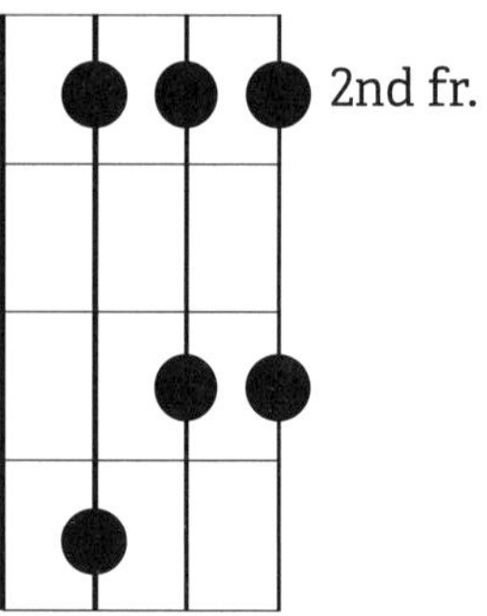

INTRO

```
               D                   G         Emi                 G
Aye, aye, aye, aye. Ooh, ooh, ooh, ooh. Aye, aye. Ooh, ooh, ooh, ooh.
```

VERSE 1

D
Needless to say, I keep it in check. She was a bad-bad, nevertheless.

G
Calling it quits now, baby, I'm a wreck. Crash at my place, baby, you're a wreck.

Emi
Needless to say, I'm keeping in check. She was a bad-bad, nevertheless.

G
Calling it quits now, baby, I'm a wreck. Crash at my place, baby, you're a wreck.

D
Thinking in a bad way, losing your grip. Screaming at my face, baby, don't trip.

G
Someone took a big L, don't know how that felt. Looking at you sideways, party on tilt.

Emi
Ooh-ooh, some things you just can't refuse.

```
            G
She wanna ride me like a cruise, and I'm not tryna lose.
```

CHORUS

D
Then you're left in the dust, unless I stuck by ya.

G
You're a sunflower, I think your love would be too much.

Emi
Or you'll be left in the dust, unless I stuck by ya.

G
You're the sunflower, you're the sunflower.

VERSE 2

D
Every time I'm leaving on ya, you don't make it easy, no.

G
Wish I could be there for you, give me a reason to.

Emi
Oh, every time I walk in now, I can hear you telling me to turn around.

G
Fighting for my trust and you won't back down, even if we gotta risk it all right now, oh.

BRIDGE

D
I know you're scared of the unknown. You don't want to be alone.

G
I know I always come and go, but it's out of my control.

REPEAT CHORUS

from SPIDER-MAN: INTO THE SPIDER-VERSE
Words and Music by Austin Richard Post, Carl Austin Rosen, Khalif Brown, Carter Lang, Louis Bell and Billy Walsh

THREE LITTLE BIRDS

Bob Marley & the Wailers

Key of Recording: A
Key of Notation: A
Form of Recording: Intro–Chorus–Verse–Chorus–Verse–Chorus
(For Use with Section 4 of the *Modern Band Bass Method*)

Song Tips:

- The bass in reggae music typically has a smooth, rounder sound. If you usually play with a pick, you might want to try using your fingers instead to give the notes a softer articulation.
- You can play just the root notes if you'd like, but if you want to give the bass line a little more movement, you can use the tab below to learn an approximation of what the bassist on the original recording plays during the choruses. If you want to experiment and come up with your own bass lines, maintain the groove by playing the root notes of each chord on the first two beats of each measure, and then add notes from the six-note groove on beat 4.

Intro:

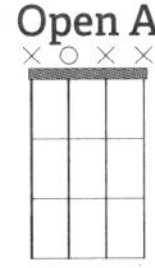

| / / / / | / / / / | / / / / | / / / / ||

1 + 2 + 3 + 4 +

Chorus:

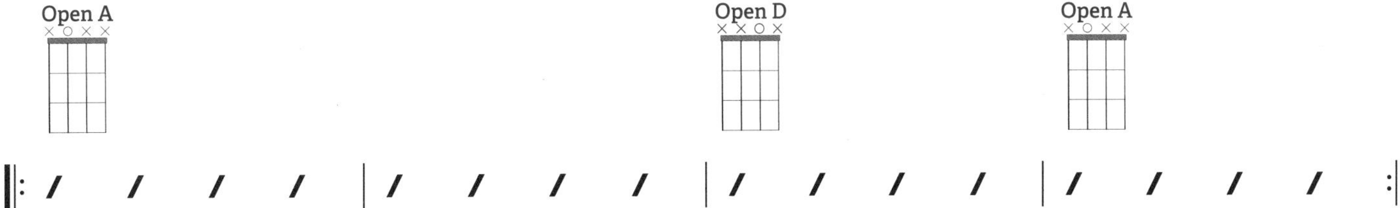

Bass Tab (Chorus):

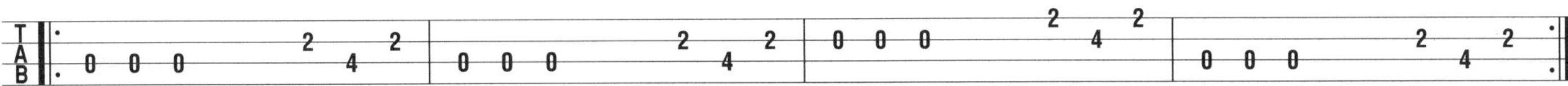

Verse:

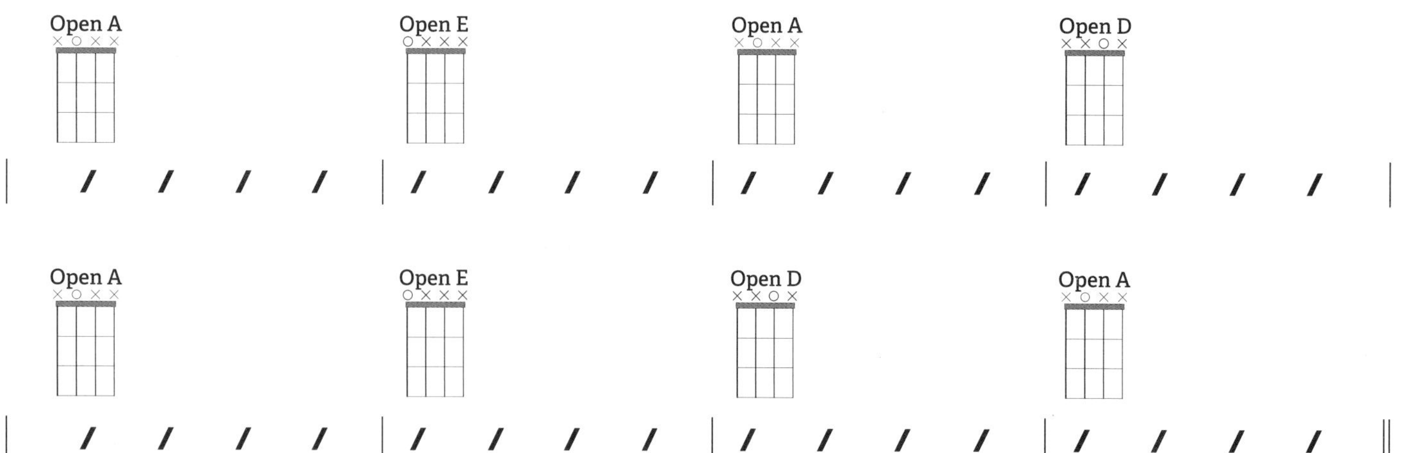

Six-Note Groove (A):

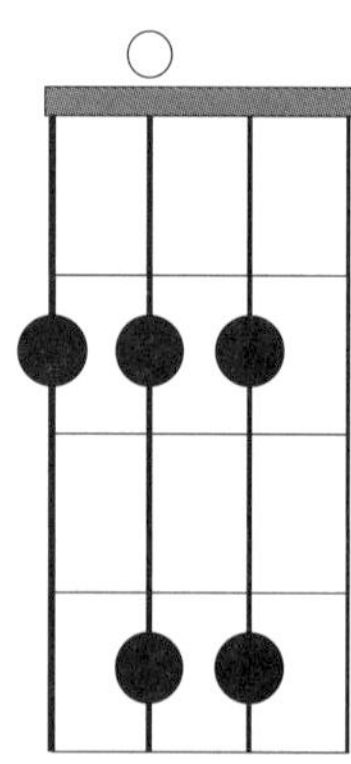

CHORUS

```
          A                                  D                                    A
Don't worry about a thing, 'cause every little thing gonna be alright.

                                               D                                    A
Singing, "Don't worry about a thing, 'cause every little thing gonna be alright."
```

VERSE

```
                 A                             E                               A             D
Rise up this morning, smile with the rising sun. Three little birds pitch by my doorstep,

               A                         E                         D                                     A
Singing sweet songs of melodies pure and true, saying, "This is my message to you-ou-ou."
```

REPEAT CHORUS

REPEAT VERSE

REPEAT CHORUS (2 TIMES)

LOVE SHINE BRIGHT

Culture

Key of Recording: B♭
Key of Notation: D
Form of Recording: Intro–Chorus–Verse 1–Chorus–Interlude–Verse 2–Chorus–Outro
(For Use with Section 4 of the *Modern Band Bass Method*)

Song Tips:

- The bass rhythmic pattern in this song is fairly "busy." If you want to challenge yourself, you can practice adding more complex rhythms.
- The length of the notes in reggae bass makes a big impact on the overall feel of the groove. Listen carefully to a recording of this song and try to match the note lengths used.
- Muting strings is also a very important technique for controlling the length of notes and maintaining a clean, accurate bass line. Be sure to stop the open D string from ringing before you play the following open E string, and vice versa. You can use both your left and your right hands to assist with string muting.

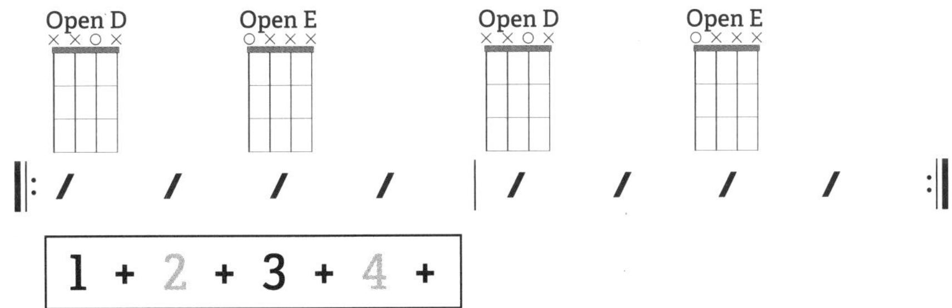

Six-Note Groove (D):

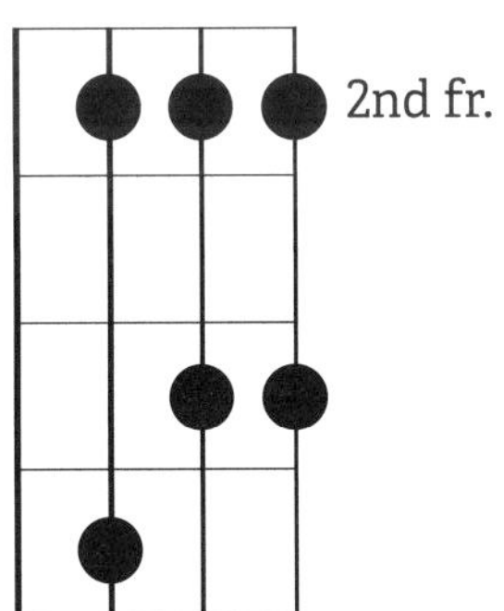

CHORUS

```
D            Emi                 D        Emi
  Love shines brighter than the morning sun.

D            Emi              D     Emi
  Love shines brighter every day.

D            Emi                 D        Emi
  Love shines brighter than the morning sun.

D            Emi              D     Emi
  Love shines brighter every day.
```

VERSE 1

```
D                Emi                 D       Emi
  We jump and wake up in the mornings,

   D               Emi                  D      Emi
It was love that caused our first heartbeat, oh yeah.

D                Emi         D                            Emi
  Check the green trees. How they bow their heads way down low sometimes

       D               Emi              D      Emi
To give thanks and praises to the Father. That's why I sing, say
```

REPEAT CHORUS

VERSE 2

```
D            Emi            D        Emi
  Check the flowers in the garden,

D                Emi            D     Emi
  See how beautiful their petals grow, oh yeah.

D         Emi            D                                 Emi
  Even the pine trees how they point their fingers to the heavens.

    D              Emi              D   Emi
And the birds, their little songs to sing. That's why I sing, say
```

REPEAT CHORUS

THE BONES

Maren Morris

Key of Recording: D
Key of Notation: G
Form of Recording: Intro–Verse 1–Chorus–Interlude–Verse 2–Chorus–Bridge–Chorus–Outro
(For Use with Section 6 of the *Modern Band Bass Method*)

Song Tips:

- The bass in this song can first be heard halfway through the first verse. However, this part is likely a rhythmic synth bass. If you want to try to emulate this sound, you can play it with a constant eighth-note pulse on the bass, changing notes on beat 1 and the "and" of beat 2 in each bar.
- The chorus of the song includes a *slash chord*. A slash chord is used to specify a bass note other than the root of the chord. In this case, the G chord in the chorus has a B as the lowest note of the chord, and the chord name includes a slash to indicate that the G chord is played with a B as the bass note: G/B ("G over B"). This alternate bass note creates a less-resolved G chord and, within the context of the chord progression, creates an ascending bass line.

Intro/Verse/Interlude:

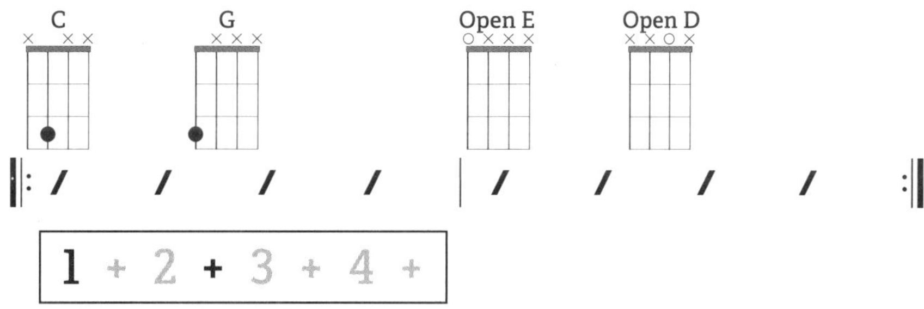

Chorus:

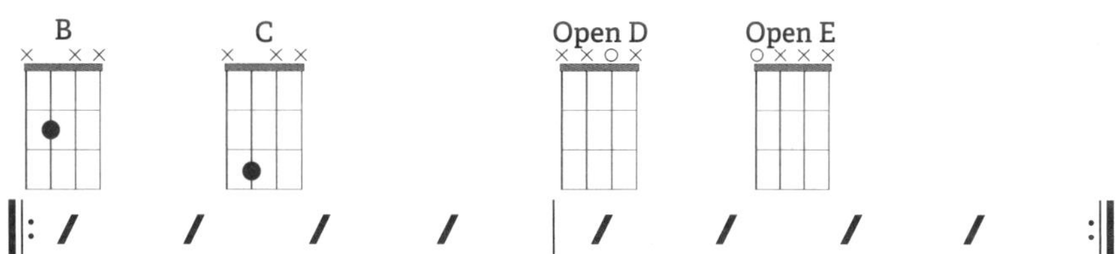

Six-Note Groove (G):

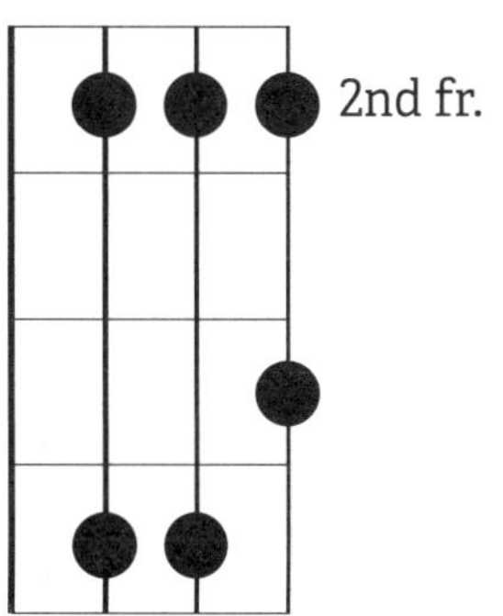

VERSE 1

            C   G   Emi   D
We're in the homestretch of the hard times.

           C   G   Emi   D
We took a hard left, but we're alright.

     C   G   Emi D
Yeah, life sure can try to put love through it, but

C   G   Emi D
  We built this right, so nothing's ever gonna move it.

CHORUS

           G   C   D   Emi
When the bones are good, the rest don't matter. Yeah, the paint could peel, the glass could shatter.

       G C   D   Emi
Let it rain 'cause you and I remain the same.

             G   C   D   Emi
When there ain't a crack in the foundation. Baby, I know any storm we're facing

     G   C   D
Will blow right over while we stay put. The house don't fall when the bones are good.

VERSE 2

       C   G   Emi   D
Call it dumb luck. But baby, you and I

            C   G   Emi   D
Can't even mess it up and though we both tried,

     C   G   Emi D
No, it don't always go the way we planned it,

       C   G   Emi   D
But the wolves came and went and we're still standing.

REPEAT CHORUS

BRIDGE

```
C              G                 Emi      D
Bones are good, the rest, baby, the rest don't really matter.

C                G                  Emi              D
Paint could peel, the glass, oh the glass, oh the glass could shatter.

C              G                 Emi  D
Bones are good, the rest, the rest don't matter.

C                G                  Emi  D
Paint could peel, the glass, the glass could shatter.
```

REPEAT CHORUS

SOMEONE YOU LOVED

Lewis Capaldi

Key of Recording: D♭
Key of Notation: C
Form of Recording: Intro–Verse 1–Chorus–Verse 2–Chorus–Bridge–Chorus–Outro
(For Use with Section 6 of the *Modern Band Bass Method*)

Song Tips:

- The original recording of this song is just voice, piano, and some faint orchestral strings. So, how do you create an arrangement that provides an opportunity for you as a bassist to play? Listen to a recording with your bandmates and brainstorm ideas. Then you can try watching covers of the song to see how other artists (such as the Jonas Brothers) have arranged it with guitar, bass, and drums.
- Bassists should focus on holding notes as long as possible in this ballad style. Work on switching smoothly between notes while giving each note its full length. Also be sure to play the notes with a gentle articulation.

Intro/Verse/Chorus:

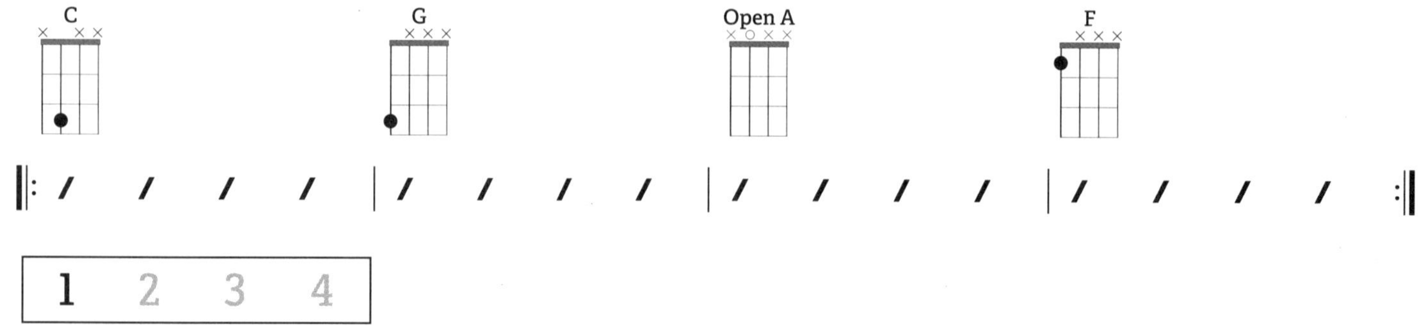

Bridge:

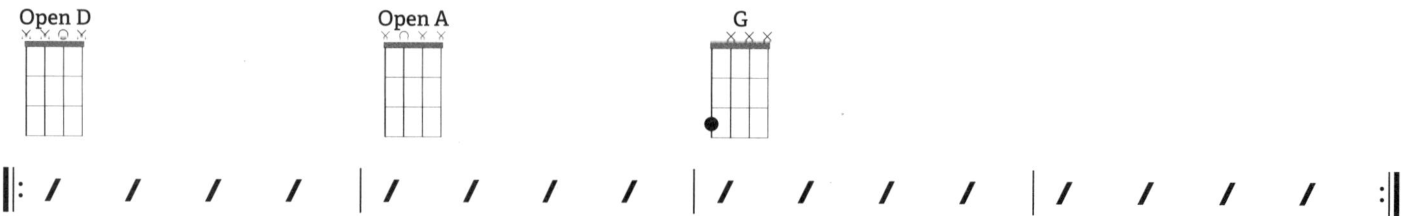

Six-Note Groove (C):

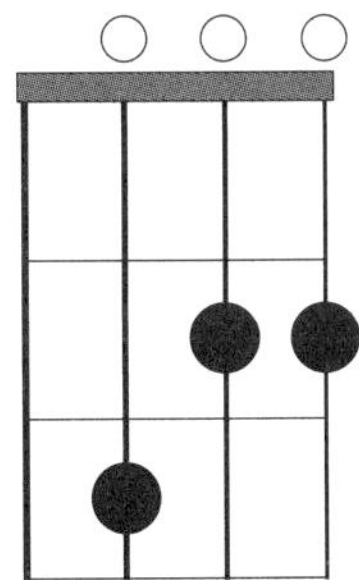

VERSE 1

C G Ami F
I'm going under, and this time, I fear there's no one to save me.

C G Ami F
This all or nothing really got a way of driving me crazy.

C G
I need somebody to heal, somebody to know,

Ami F
Somebody to have, somebody to hold.

C G
It's easy to say, but it's never the same.

Ami F
I guess I kinda liked the way you numbed all the pain.

CHORUS

C G
Now the day bleeds into nightfall,

Ami F
And you're not here to get me through it all.

C G
I let my guard down, and then you pulled the rug.

Ami F
I was getting kinda used to being someone you loved.

VERSE 2

```
C                                        G                                              Ami       F
  I'm going under, and this time, I fear there's no one to turn to.

C                                        G                                              Ami       F
  This all or nothing way of loving got me sleeping without you.

                                              C                         G
Now, I need somebody to know, somebody to heal,

                      Ami                                   F
Somebody to have, just to know how it feels.

                C                              G
It's easy to say, but it's never the same.

                  Ami                                  F
I guess I kinda liked the way you help me escape.
```

REPEAT CHORUS

BRIDGE

```
      Dmi             Ami                              G
And I tend to close my eyes when it hurts sometimes.

                        Dmi           Ami                                  G
I fall into your arms. I'll be safe in your sound 'til I come back around.
```

REPEAT CHORUS (2 TIMES)

ÉCHAME LA CULPA

Luis Fonsi and Demi Lovato

Key of Recording: C
Key of Notation: C
Form of Recording: Intro–Verse 1–Chorus–Verse 2–Chorus–Bridge–Verse 2–Chorus–Bridge
(For Use with Section 7 of the *Modern Band Bass Method*)

Song Tips:

- Bilingual songs in Spanish and English have become increasingly popular in the United States as Spanish-speaking and bilingual artists like Luis Fonsi, Bad Bunny, Selena Gomez, Karol G, Daddy Yankee, Pitbull, Ricky Martin, Carlos Santana, Shakira, Camila Cabello, and Lin-Manuel Miranda have grown in popularity and collaborated with English-speaking artists such as Demi Lovato and Justin Bieber. What makes a bilingual song different from one sung in just one language? What does each artist bring to the song? Does it feel like each artist's style can be heard throughout the song? Many people listen to songs in languages they don't speak. Why might they do that?
- This is an uptempo song. It could be easy to get lost or overwhelmed trying to play through the song at tempo. Take some time during rehearsal to build up muscle memory at a much slower tempo before trying to play it at the speed of the original recording.
- Bassists should pay extra attention to the length of bass notes in the recording and work with the drummers to lock in the Latin pop style of this song.
- The bass line is shown below in notation and tab, and is a typical pattern in cumbia music. It is built from *arpeggiated chords*, which are chords played one note at a time instead of all at once. So, the notes that comprise the bass line are tones from the chords being played by the harmony instruments (guitar, keyboard, and ukulele).

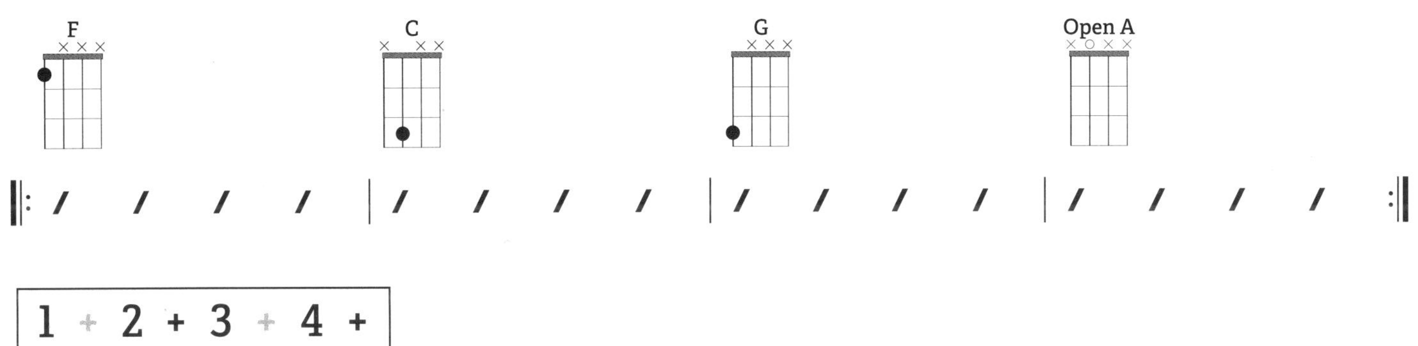

Bass Tab:

Six-Note Groove (C):

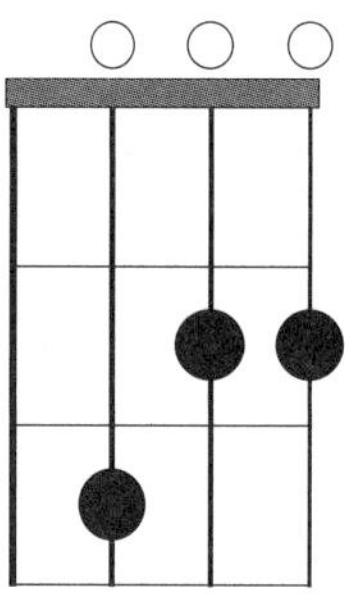

VERSE 1

F C
Tengo en esta historia algo que confesar. Ya entendí muy bien que fue lo que pasó.

G Ami
Y aunque duela tanto tengo que aceptar. Que tú no eres la mala, que el malo soy yo.

F C
No me conociste nunca de verdad. Ya se fue la magia que te enamoró.

G Ami
Y es que no quisiera estar en tu lugar. Porque tu error sólo fue conocerme.

CHORUS

F C
No eres tú, no eres tú, no eres tú, soy yo (soy yo). No te quiero hacer sufrir,

G Ami
Es mejor olvidar y dejarlo. Así (así), échame la culpa.

F C
No eres tú, no eres tú, no eres tú, soy yo (soy yo). No te quiero hacer sufrir,

G Ami
Es mejor olvidar y dejarlo. Así (así), échame la culpa.

VERSE 2

F C
Okay, I don't really, really wanna fight anymore. I don't really, really wanna fake it no more.

G Ami
Play me like The Beatles, baby, just "Let It Be." So come and put the blame on me, yeah.

F C
I don't really, really wanna fight anymore. I don't really, really wanna fake it no more.

G Ami
Play me like The Beatles, baby, just "Let It Be." So come and put the blame on me, yeah.

REPEAT CHORUS

BRIDGE

F C
Solamente te falta un beso. Solamente te falta un beso.

G Ami
Ese beso que siempre te prometí. Échame la culpa.

F C
Solamente te falta un beso. Solamente te falta un beso.

G Ami
Ese beso que siempre te prometí. Échame la culpa.

REPEAT VERSE 2

REPEAT CHORUS

REPEAT BRIDGE

OJITOS LINDOS

Bad Bunny and Bomba Estéreo

Key of Recording: F#
Key of Notation: G
Form of Recording: Intro–Verse 1–Pre-Chorus–Chorus–Verse 2–Chorus–Interlude–Verse 3–Verse 4–Pre-Chorus–Chorus
(For Use with Section 7 of the *Modern Band Bass Method*)

Song Tips:

- Most of the accompaniment for this song is played as whole notes. However, in creating an arrangement, you can play a variety of rhythms in different sections to build or lower the intensity, or change the style of the song.
- The bass part could be expanded by playing the same notes in higher *octaves*. Based on the steps of a scale, an octave is the distance of eight notes higher or lower than a note with the same name. Check out the note diagrams below. You can play the same four notes from the song (C, E, D, and A) one octave higher. Explore playing the notes in different octaves at different points in the song and try mixing them up in various ways. Reflect on the effects that higher or lower tones have on the sound and feel of the music.

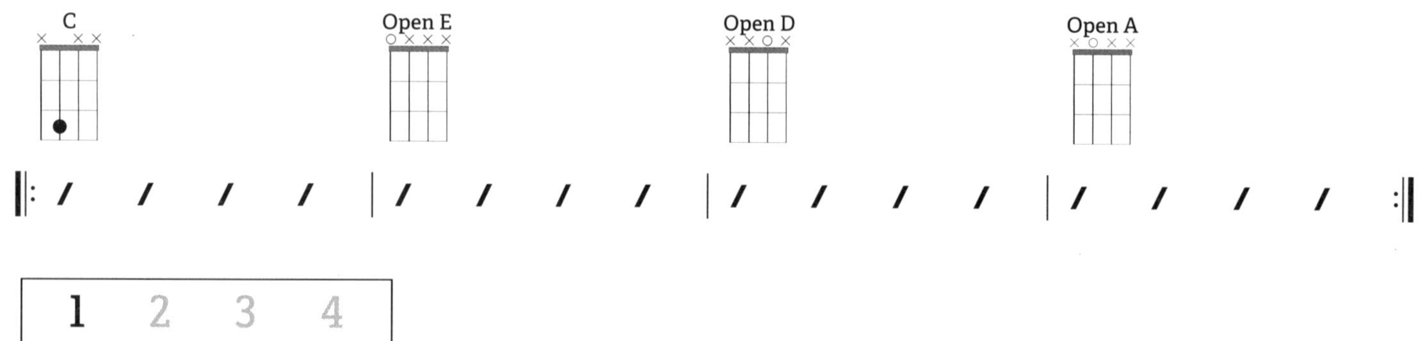

Octave Notes:

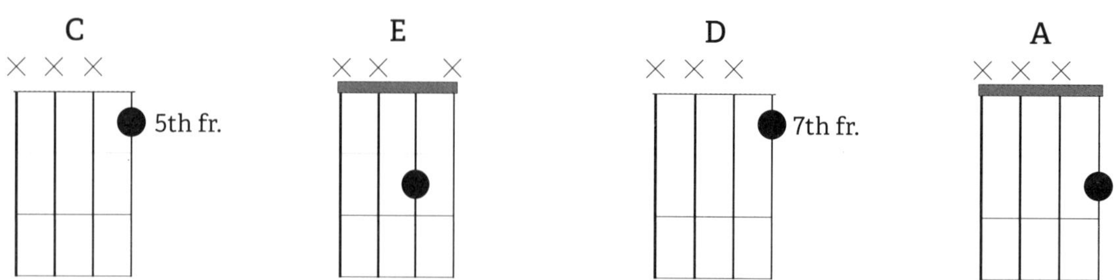

Six-Note Groove (G):

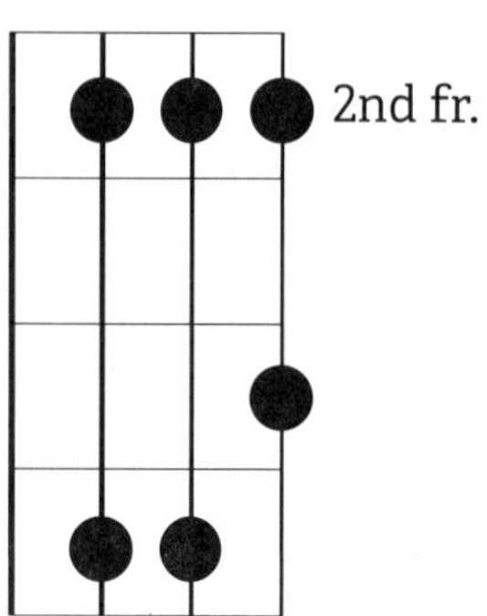

VERSE 1

            C   Emi   D   Ami
Hace mucho tiempo le hago caso al corazón,

           C   Emi   D   Ami
Y pasan los días, los meses, pensando en tu olor.

             C   Emi   D   Ami
Ha llegado el tiempo para usar la razón,

             C   Emi   D   Ami
Ante' que sea tarde y sin querer me parta en do'.

PRE-CHORUS

             C   Emi   D   Ami
Antes de que salga el sol y hunde el acelerador. Que vaya sin freno y pierda el control.

             C   Emi   D   Ami
Nada más seremos dos, tú y yo acariciándonos. En medio del tiempo, sin decir adiós.

CHORUS

      C   Emi   D   Ami
Y sólo mírame con esos ojitos lindos, que con eso yo estoy bien.

C   Emi   D   Ami
  Hoy he vuelto a nacer.

VERSE 2

      C   Emi   D   Ami
Hace tiempo que no agarro a nadie de la mano,

      C   Emi   D   Ami
Hace tiempo que no envío "Buenos días, te amo."

                      C   Emi   D   Ami
Pero tú me tiene' enredao, me envolví. Iba por mi camino y me perdí.

               C   Emi   D   Ami
Mi mirada cambió cuando tus ojos vi. Bye-bye a lo' culo', ni me despedí.

        C   Emi   D   Ami
Yo no te busqué, no, chocamo' en el trayecto. Con tú alma es lo que yo

    C   Emi   D   Ami
Conecto. Tranquila, no tiene que ser perfecto, no.

            C   Emi   D   Ami
Aquí no existe el pecado y equivocarse es bonito.

        C   Emi   D   Ami
Los errores son placeres, igual que to' tus besito'.

REPEAT CHORUS (2 TIMES)

INTERLUDE

C Emi D Ami
Tú y yo, tú y yo, tú y yo. (Tú y yo, tú y yo.)

C Emi D Ami
Tú y yo, tú y yo, tú y yo.

VERSE 3

C Emi D Ami
Yo no me dejo llevar de nadie. Yo sólo me dejo llevar de tu sonrisa. Y del lunar cerquita de tú

C Emi D Ami
Boca. Si yo estoy loco, tú estás loquita. Pero, baby, como tú no hay

C Emi D Ami
Otra, no. Quiero regalarte girasoles.

C Emi D Ami
Ir pa' la playa y buscarte caracoles. Cuando estoy contigo, yo no miro el Rolex. Vamo' a bailar

C Emi D Ami
Doscientas canciones. Nadie me pone como tú me pones.

C Emi D Ami
Hmm-mm-mm, hm-mm hm-mm, hmm-mm. Hmm-mm-mm, hm-mm hm-mm, hmm-mm.

VERSE 4

C Emi D Ami
Yo le hablo a Dios y tú eres su respuesta. Aprendí que los momentos lindos nunca cuestan,

C Emi D Ami
Cómo cuándo me regalas tú mirada. Y el sol su puesta, y el sol su puesta.

C Emi D Ami
Cuando estoy encima de ti, de ti. Mami, yo me olvido de todo, de todo.

C Emi D Ami
No hace falta nadie aquí. Solamente tú y yo.

REPEAT PRE-CHORUS

REPEAT CHORUS (2 TIMES)

BAD BLOOD

Taylor Swift

Key of Recording: G
Key of Notation: G
Form of Recording: Chorus–Verse 1–Pre-Chorus–Chorus–Verse 2–Pre-Chorus–Chorus–Bridge–Chorus
(For Use with Section 8 of the *Modern Band Bass Method*)

Song Tips:

- The main elements of this song are the vocals and the percussive elements. If you and your bandmates want to feature members of the band other than the singer and drummers, you can try reimagining the song in a different genre. You can find a variety of covers on YouTube that recreate the song within different genres, such as acoustic and rock.
- This song has an overall angry tone. You might want to experiment by adding distortion to your bass sound to match the emotional tone of the lyrics. Some bass amps will have an overdrive or distortion feature. If yours doesn't, it might have a gain and a volume control. To get a distorted sound, turn the volume down and the gain up. The higher the gain, the louder and more distorted the sound. Since gain also increases the volume, we turn the volume down first to protect everyone's ears!
- Due to the punchier style of this song, you may want to use a pick to get more attack on each note.
- The chorus at the beginning of the song is sung without any chords, but we have still included the chord names in the correct spots for reference. The same happens for the first half of each chorus later in the song.

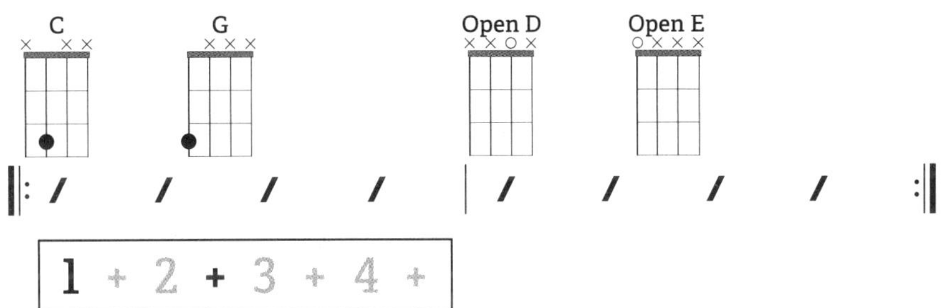

Six-Note Groove (G):

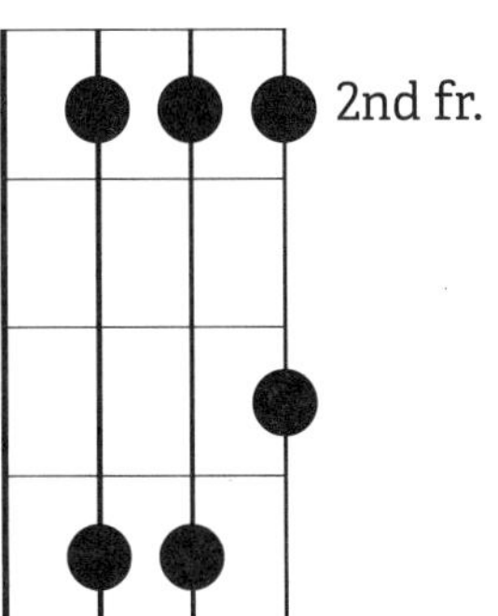

CHORUS

```
             C              G                   D            Emi
'Cause baby, now we got bad blood. You know it used to be mad love.

          C                     G             D              Emi
So take a look what you've done, 'cause baby, now we got bad blood, hey!

C                G                 D                Emi
Now we got problems, and I don't think we can solve 'em.

            C           G             D              Emi
You made a really deep cut, and baby, now we got bad blood, hey!
```

VERSE 1

```
C       G                D          Emi
Did you have to do this? I was thinking that you could be trusted.

C       G            D               Emi
Did you have to ruin what was shiny? Now it's all rusted.

C       G               D              Emi
Did you have to hit me where I'm weak? Baby, I couldn't breathe.

     C    G           D                  Emi
And rub it in so deep, salt in the wound like you're laughing right at me.
```

PRE-CHORUS

```
C    G        D  Emi                C       G          D
  Oh, it's so sad to think about the good times. You and I.
```

CHORUS

```
             C              G                   D            Emi
'Cause baby, now we got bad blood. You know it used to be mad love.

          C                     G             D              Emi
So take a look what you've done, 'cause baby, now we got bad blood, hey!

C                G                 D                Emi
Now we got problems, and I don't think we can solve 'em.

            C           G             D              Emi
You made a really deep cut, and baby, now we got bad blood, hey!
```

VERSE 2

```
C         G                          D                 Emi
Did you think we'd be fine? Still got scars on my back from your knife,

   C          G                  D                         Emi
So, don't think it's in the past. These kinds of wounds, they last and they last.

     C      G                          D                  Emi
Now, did you think it all through? All these things will catch up to you.

     C       G                              D                      Emi
And time can heal but this won't. So, if you're coming my way, just don't.
```

REPEAT PRE-CHORUS

REPEAT CHORUS

BRIDGE

```
C                 G                 D            Emi
Band-aids don't fix bullet holes. You say "sorry" just for show.

       C            G                         D    Emi
If you live like that, you live with ghosts.

C                 G                 D            Emi
Band-aids don't fix bullet holes. You say "sorry" just for show.

       C            G                         D    Emi
If you live like that, you live with ghosts.

       C             G
If you love like that, blood runs cold.
```

REPEAT CHORUS (2 TIMES)

BAILANDO

Enrique Iglesias ft. Descemer Bueno & Gente de Zona

Key of Recording: E Minor
Key of Notation: E Minor
Form of Recording: Intro–Verse 1–Chorus–Bridge–Interlude–Verse 2–Chorus–Bridge–Interlude
(For Use with Section 8 of the *Modern Band Bass Method*)

Song Tips:

- Most of this song uses the same chord progression. Challenge yourself and your bandmates to come up with creative ways to keep the performance interesting and engaging. This might mean having different instrument groups drop out or slightly changing the comping pattern throughout the performance.
- This song includes *sixteenth-note* rhythms. To get this feel, try counting the beats twice as fast as usual. Rather than breaking the beats up into groups of two (1 + 2 + 3 + 4 +), you can think of them in groups of four (1 e + a, 2 e + a, 3 e + a, 4 e + a). Check out the rhythm pattern below, which is broken up into the sixteenth-note counting pattern. Practice this slowly while counting out loud to help feel this new rhythmic pattern. Compare the rhythms of the bass line notation below to the rhythm pattern grid for this song—they're the same!

Intro/Verse/Bridge/Interlude:

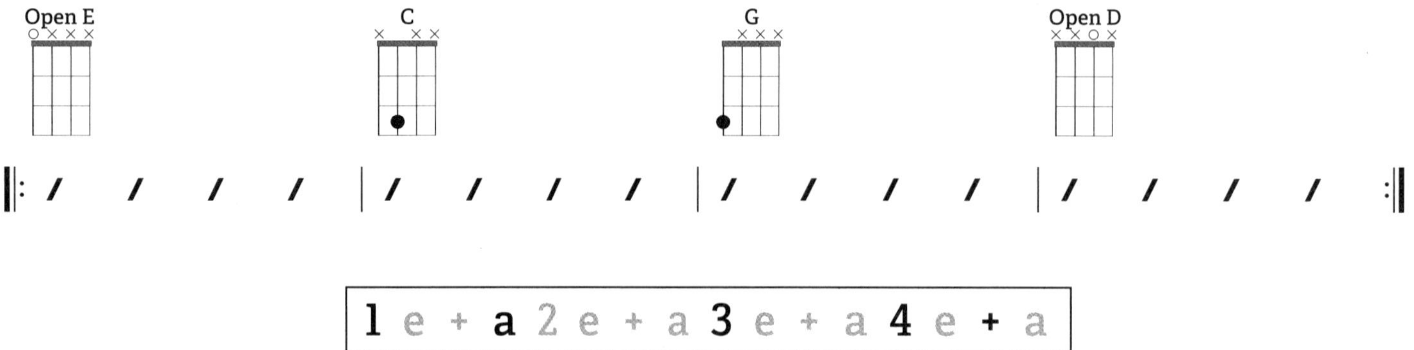

Chorus:

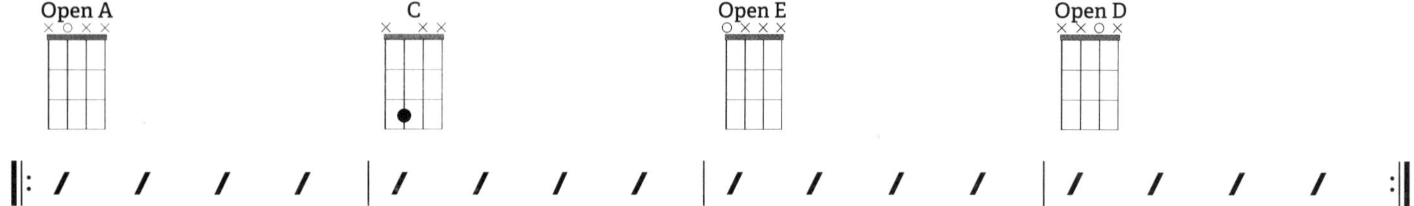

Bass Tab (Intro/Verse/Bridge/Interlude):

Six-Note Groove (E Minor):

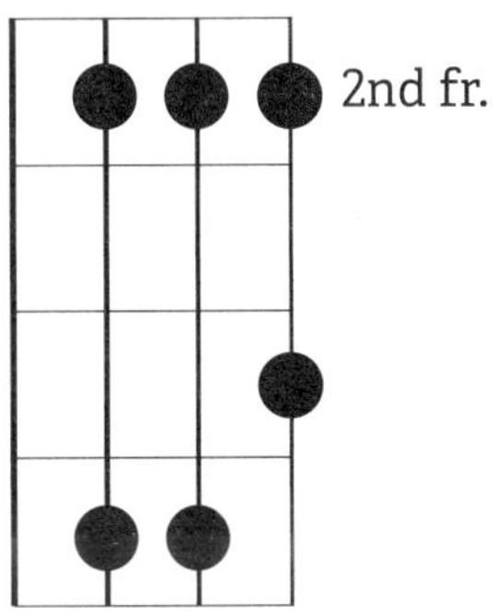

VERSE 1

Emi C G D
Yo te miro y se me corta la respiración. Cuando tú me miras se me sube el corazón.

Emi C G D
Y en un silencio tu mirada dice mil palabras. La noche en la que te suplico que no salga el sol.

CHORUS

Ami C
Bailando (bailando), bailando (bailando).

Emi D
Tu cuerpo y el mío llenando el vacío, subiendo y bajando.

Ami C
Bailando (bailando), bailando (bailando).

Emi D
Ese fuego por dentro me está enloqueciendo, me va saturando.

BRIDGE

```
                  Emi                                                  C
Con tu física y tu química, también tu anatomía. La cerveza y el tequila, y tu boca con la mía.

              G                                   D
Ya no puedo más (ya no puedo más). Ya no puedo más (ya no puedo más).

               Emi                                   C
Con esta melodía, tu color, tu fantasía. Con tu filosofía mi cabeza está vacía.

              G                                   D
Ya no puedo más (ya no puedo más). Ya no puedo más (ya no puedo más).

                   Emi                          C
Yo quiero estar contigo, vivir contigo, bailar contigo, tener contigo.

             G                               D
Una noche loca (una noche loca). Ay, besar tu boca (besar tu boca).

                   Emi                          C
Yo quiero estar contigo, vivir contigo, bailar contigo, tener contigo.

             G                     D
Una noche loca, con tremenda nota.
```

INTERLUDE

```
          Emi           C             G              D
Oh-oh-oh-oh. Oh-oh-oh-oh. Oh-oh-oh-oh. Oh-oh-oh-oh.
```

VERSE 2

```
Emi                                            C   G                                D
  Tú me miras y me llevas a otra dimensión. Tus latidos aceleran a mi corazón.

Emi                                          C          G                                D
  Qué ironía del destino no poder tocarte, abrazarte, y sentir la magia de tu olor.
```

REPEAT CHORUS

REPEAT BRIDGE

REPEAT INTERLUDE (3 TIMES)

COLD HEART (PNAU Remix)

Elton John and Dua Lipa

Key of Recording: B♭ Minor
Key of Notation: A Minor
Form of Recording: Intro–Verse–Pre-Chorus–Chorus–Pre-Chorus–Chorus–Pre-Chorus–Chorus–Outro
(For Use with Section 9 of the *Modern Band Bass Method*)

Song Tips:

- "Cold Heart" uses musical content from the 1972 Elton John hit "Rocket Man." Listen to that and other songs by Elton John. How is it similar or different from modern pop songs, like "Cold Heart"? How has popular music changed in the last 50 years? How has it stayed the same? Every artist you listen to today was musically inspired by other artists. What musical artists have influenced you? Who do you think has inspired your favorite musical artists?
- The original bass line is quite syncopated and could prove challenging. It includes octaves and some jumps around the fretboard. Check out the notation and tab below. You can simplify the bass line by just playing the root notes with single eighth notes on the upbeats rather than sixteenth notes.

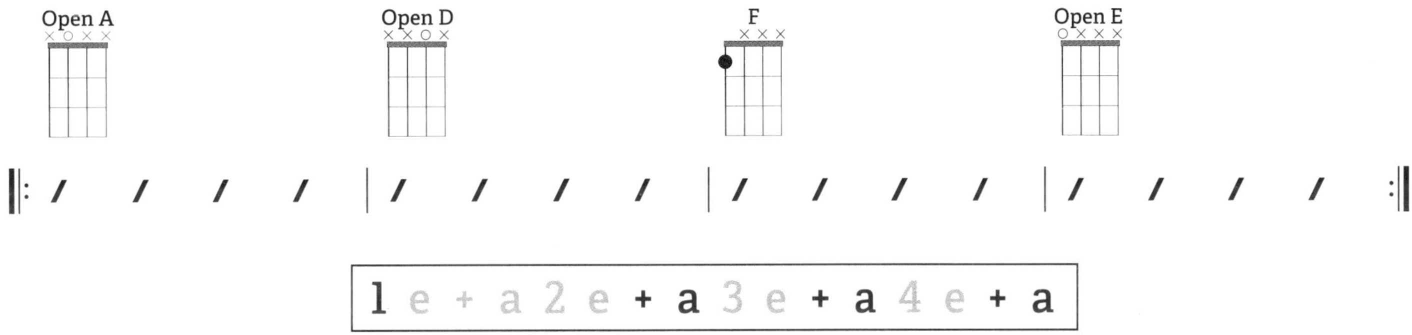

Bass Tab:

A Minor Pentatonic Scale:

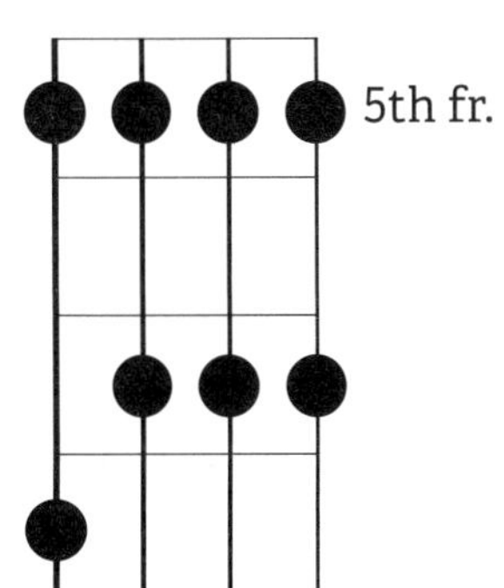

VERSE

Ami Dmi F Emi
It's a human sign when things go wrong.

Ami Dmi F Emi
When the scent of her lingers and temptation's strong.

PRE-CHORUS

Ami Dmi F Emi
Cold, cold heart, hard done by you.

Ami Dmi F Emi
Some things lookin' better, baby, just passing through.

CHORUS

Ami Dmi F Emi
And I think it's gonna be a long, long time 'til touchdown brings me 'round again to find

Ami Dmi F Emi
I'm not the man they think I am at home. Oh, no, no, no.

Ami Dmi F Emi
And this is what I should have said,

Ami Dmi F Emi
Well, I thought it, but I kept it hid.

REPEAT PRE-CHORUS

REPEAT CHORUS

REPEAT PRE-CHORUS

REPEAT CHORUS

ADORE YOU

Harry Styles

Key of Recording: C Minor
Key of Notation: E Minor
Form of Recording: Intro–Verse 1–Pre-Chorus 1–Chorus–Verse 2–Pre-Chorus 2–Chorus–Bridge–Chorus
(For Use with Section 9 of the *Modern Band Bass Method*)

Song Tips:

- "Adore You" focuses primarily on a basic groove to carry the lead vocals. Establishing this groove, which features elements of disco, funk, and pop music, is an important first step in preparing for this performance.
- The original bass line of this song utilizes octaves to achieve a funk sound. There are several ways to approach this. You could play only the root notes in their lowest octave, as illustrated in the note diagrams and staff below. Or you could alternate octaves by switching between the lowest roots and their octave notes. Lastly, refer to the bass tab below to perform it as it's played in the original recording.

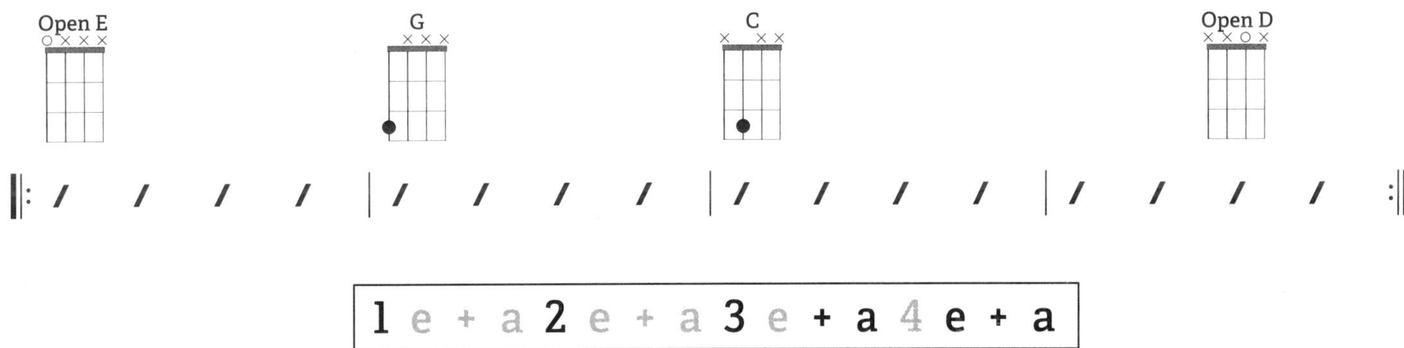

1 e + a 2 e + a 3 e + a 4 e + a

Bass Tab:

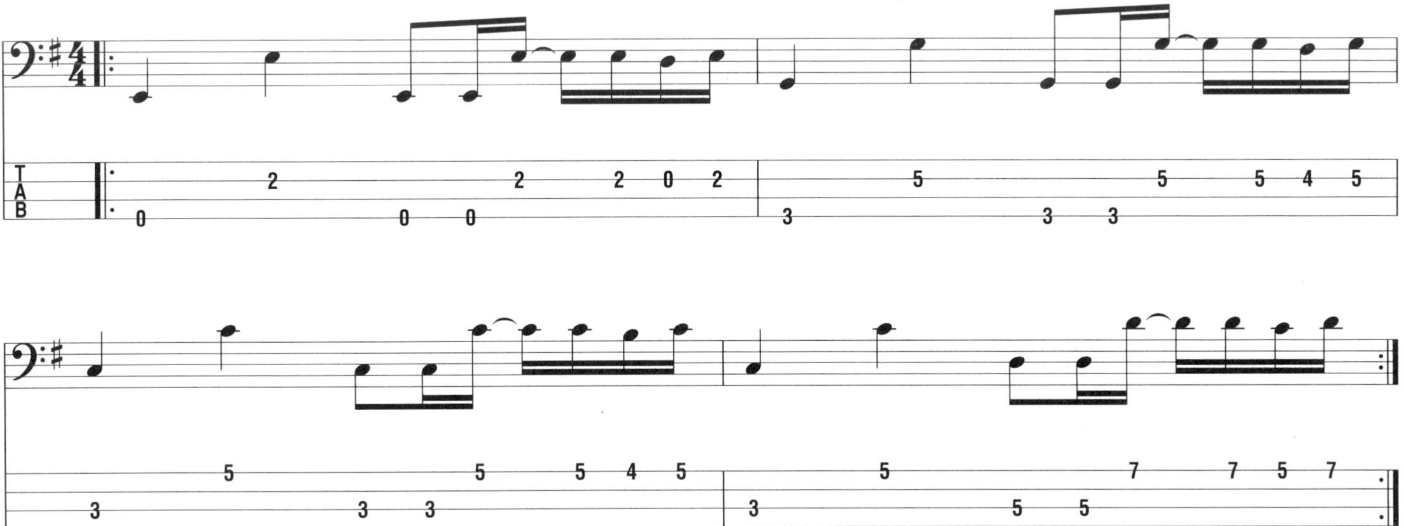

E Minor Pentatonic Scale:

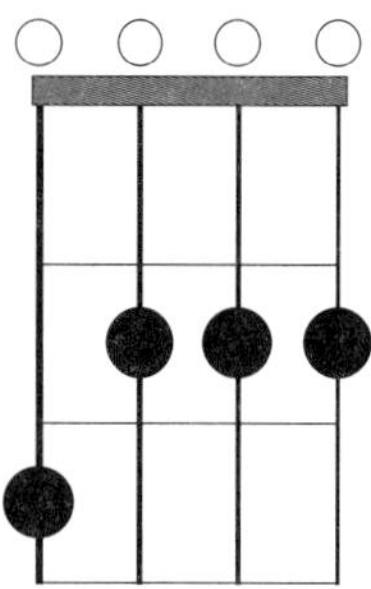

VERSE 1

Emi   G   C   D
  Walk in your rainbow paradise (paradise).

Emi   G   C   D
  Strawberry lipstick state of mind (state of mind).

Emi   G   C   D
  I get so lost inside your eyes. Would you believe it?

PRE-CHORUS 1

Emi   G
You don't have to say you love me. You don't have to say nothing.

C   D
You don't have to say you're mine.

CHORUS

**   Emi   G   C   D**
Honey (ah-ah-ah), I'd walk through fire for you. Just let me adore you.

**   Emi   G   C   D**
Oh, honey (ah-ah-ah), I'd walk through fire for you. Just let me adore you.

**   Emi   G   C   D**
Like it's the only thing I'll ever do. Like it's the only thing I'll ever do.

VERSE 2

Emi   G   C   D
  Your wonder, under summer skies.

Emi   G   C   D
  Brown skin and lemon over ice. Would you believe it?

PRE-CHORUS 2

Emi **G**
You don't have to say you love me. I just wanna tell you something.

C **D**
Lately, you've been on my mind.

REPEAT CHORUS

BRIDGE

Emi **G**
It's the only thing I'll ever do. It's the only thing I'll ever do.

C **D**
It's the only thing I'll ever do. It's the only thing I'll ever do.

Emi **G**
It's the only thing I'll ever do. It's the only thing I'll ever do.

C **D**
It's the only thing I'll ever do. It's the only thing I'll ever do.

REPEAT CHORUS (2 TIMES)

DEATH BED (Coffee for Your Head)

Powfu ft. Beabadoobee

Key of Recording: Between C and C#
Key of Notation: C
Form of Recording: Chorus–Verse 1–Chorus–Verse 2–Chorus
(For Use with Section 10 of the *Modern Band Bass Method*)

Song Tips:

- The pitch of this song's original recording doesn't align with standard tuning. Unless your bass is specially tuned, playing along with the original song will sound out of tune, though you can get close by playing in C.
- "Death Bed (Coffee for Your Head)" samples the Beabadoobee song "Coffee." Listen to the original song for inspiration and to determine what is different between "Coffee" and "Death Bed (Coffee for Your Head)."
- The bass alone can affect the overall style and feel of a song. Be creative and intentional with how you play and arrange the bass part—add your own spin to it!

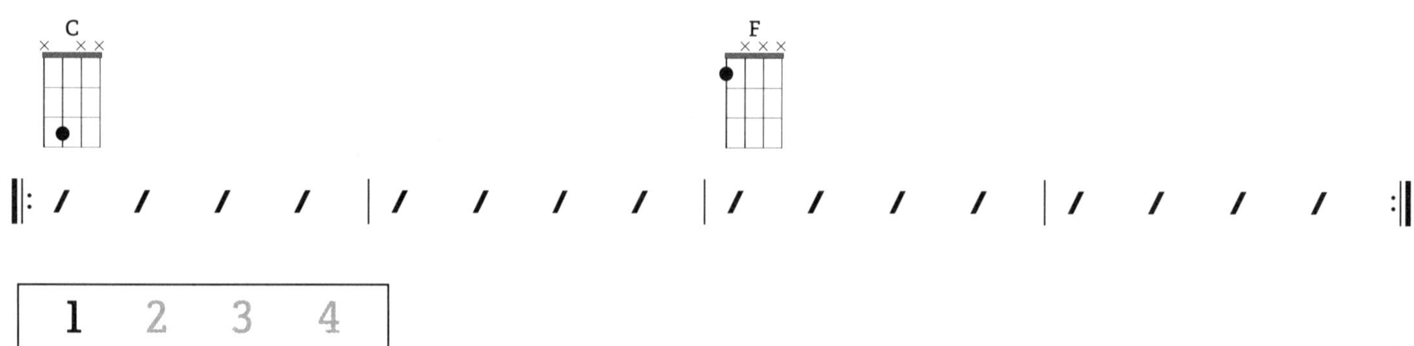

C Major Pentatonic Scale:

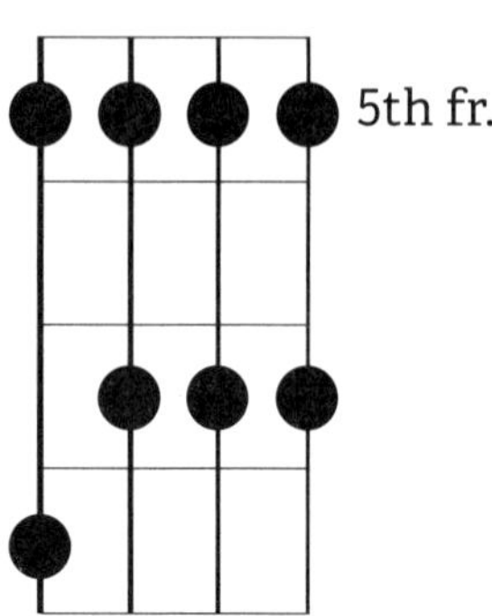

CHORUS

C   Cmaj7
Don't stay awake for too long, don't go to bed.

F   F7
I'll make a cup of coffee for your head. It'll get you up and going out of bed.

VERSE 1

C
Yeah, I don't wanna fall asleep, I don't wanna pass away.

Cmaj7
I been thinking of our future 'cause I'll never see those days.

F
I don't know why this has happened, but I probably deserve it.

F7
I tried to do my best, but you know that I'm not perfect.

C
I been praying for forgiveness; you've been praying for my health.

Cmaj7
When I leave this Earth, hopin' you'll find someone else.

F
'Cause yeah, we still young, there's so much we haven't done,

F7
Getting married, start a family, watch your husband with his son.

C
I wish it could be me, but I won't make it out this bed.

Cmaj7
I hope I go to heaven so I see you once again.

F
My life was kinda short, but I got so many blessings.

F7
Happy you were mine; it sucks that it's all ending.

REPEAT CHORUS (2 TIMES)

VERSE 2

C
I'm happy that you here with me, I'm sorry if I tear up.

Cmaj7
When me and you were younger, you would always make me cheer up.

F
Taking goofy videos and walking through the park,

F7
You would jump into my arms every time you heard a bark.

C
Cuddle in your sheets, sing me sound asleep,

Cmaj7
And sneak out through your kitchen at exactly one o' three.

F
Sundays, went to church, on Mondays, watched a movie.

F7
Soon you'll be alone, sorry that you have to lose me.

REPEAT CHORUS (5 TIMES)

EVERYTHING IS EVERYTHING

Lauryn Hill

Key of Recording: E Minor
Key of Notation: E Minor
Form of Recording: Intro–Chorus 1–Verse 1–Chorus 2–Verse 2–Chorus 3–Verse 3–Chorus 2–Chorus 3–Outro
(For Use with Section 10 of the *Modern Band Bass Method*)

Song Tips:

- The trickiest part of performing this song might be counting the chord hits. They're spaced out and syncopated. However, after you've learned them once through, you've learned them for the whole song. You might want to start learning these hits by counting and clapping or by using body percussion before adding your bass and playing the notes. Be sure to follow the rhythm patterns shown under each measure!
- You can choose to play along with these chord hits using the root notes and rhythm patterns shown with the staff here, or you can play the bass line from the song, which is also given below in notation and tab. Notice how the rhythms and notes of the tabbed bass line are similar to the chord hits, but slightly different, with some added passing tones and reinforcing rhythms.
- For improvising or adding your own groove, use the E blues scale. This scale is first introduced in Section 11 of the *Modern Band Bass Method*, but here is a chance to learn it early!

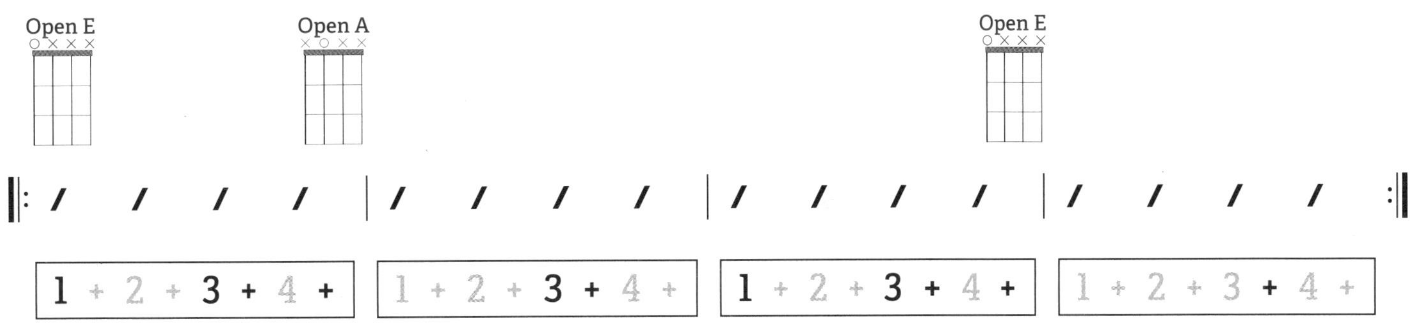

Bass Tab:

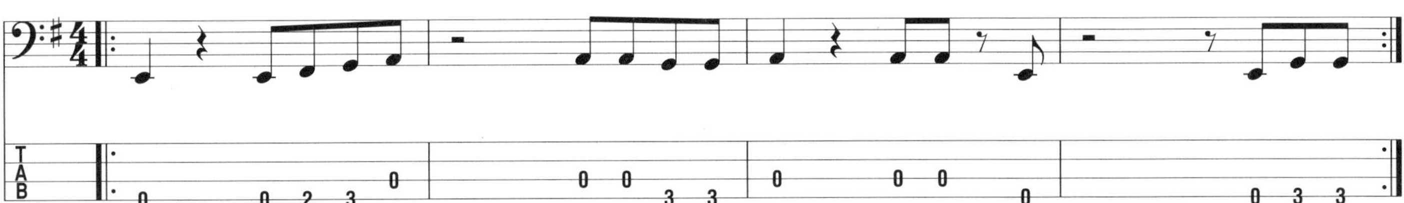

E Blues Scale:

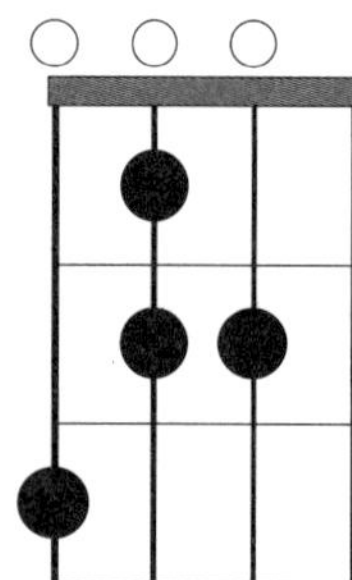

CHORUS 1

```
E7         Ami                                E7
  Everything is everything; what is meant to be, will be.

         Ami                                          E7
After winter, must come spring; change, it comes eventually.

         Ami                                E7
Everything is everything; what is meant to be, will be.

         Ami                                          E7
After winter, must come spring; change, it comes eventually.
```

VERSE 1

```
E7                    Ami                     E7
  I wrote these words for everyone who struggles in their youth,

                 Ami                  E7
Who won't accept deceptionin' instead of what is truth.

                     Ami                        E7
It seems we lose the game before we even start to play.

                     Ami                         E7
Who made these rules? We're so confused, easily led astray.
```

CHORUS 2

```
                   E7              Ami                     E7
Let me tell ya that everything is everything, everything is everything.

            Ami                                    E7
After winter must come spring; everything is everything.
```

VERSE 2

```
E7                            Ami
I philosophy, possibly speak tongues, beat drums, Abyssinian, street Baptist,

                                          E7
Rap this in fine linen. From the beginning, my practice extending across the atlas.

                                             Ami
I begat this, flippin' in the ghetto on a dirty mattress. You can't match this rapper slash actress,

                                 E7
More powerful than two Cleopatras; bomb graffiti on the tomb of Nefertiti.

                                          Ami
MCs ain't ready to take it to the Serengeti. My rhymes is heavy like the mind of Sister Betty.

                                         E7
L. Boogie spars with stars and constellations, then came down for a little conversation.

                                      Ami
Adjacent to the king, fear no human being, roll with cherubims to Nassau Coliseum.

                                               E7
Now here this mixture, where hip hop meets scripture. Develop a negative into a positive picture.
```

CHORUS 3

```
E7                 Ami                                E7
  Now, everything is everything; what is meant to be, will be.

                Ami                                          E7
And after winter, must come spring; change, it comes eventually.
```

VERSE 3

```
E7                   Ami                                                        E7
  Sometimes it seems, we'll touch that dream, but things come slow or not at all.

                   Ami                                            E7
And the ones on top won't make it stop, so convinced that they might fall.

                         Ami                              E7
Let's love ourselves and we can't fail to make a better situation.

          Ami                                          E7
Tomorrow, our seeds will grow, all we need is dedication.
```

REPEAT CHORUS 2

REPEAT CHORUS 3

LIP GLOSS

Lil Mama

Key of Recording: N/A
Key of Notation: N/A
Form of Recording: Intro–Chorus–Verse 1–Chorus–Verse 2–Chorus–Bridge 1–Verse 3–Bridge 2–Chorus–Outro
(For Use with Section 10 of the *Modern Band Bass Method*)

Song Tips:

- This song has no melodic or harmonic accompaniment. The focus is all on rhythm and lyrics! So every person, regardless of their typical instrument, should learn the groove of the song using body percussion. Once you are comfortable, you can freestyle rapped or sung lyrics, add riffs/chords, create background vocals or melodies for the chorus, or anything else that comes to mind. All of that being said, this is also a great example of how a song can remain simple yet still be impactful.
- For the purposes of the song form, the lyrics "What you know 'bout me?" are part of the chorus (or "hook"). The sections with a.sung melody are referred to as the bridge.
- The percussion parts can be performed as group body percussion, or they can be broken down into the low and high parts, as shown below.

Low Percussion (Kick Drum):

High Percussion (Hand Clap/Snare Drum):

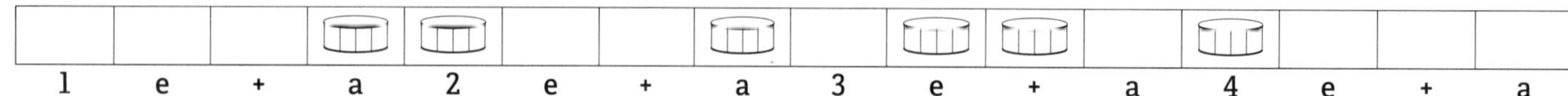

Low & High Percussion (All Together):

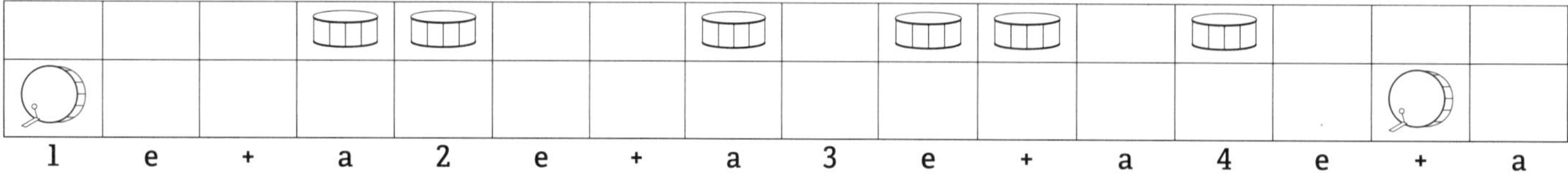

INTRO

Hello. Yeah! Uh-huh.

(It's poppin', it's poppin', it's poppin', it's poppin'.)

Okay, yeah. I gotta ask 'em, 'cause if I don't...

(It's poppin', it's poppin', it's poppin', it's poppin'.)

I don't know. Let's go!

CHORUS

What you know 'bout me? What you, what you know 'bout me?

What you know 'bout me? What you, what you know?

They say my lip gloss is cool; my lip gloss be poppin'.

I'm standing at my locker, and all the boys keep stoppin'.

What you know 'bout me? What you, what you know 'bout me?

What you know 'bout me? What you, what you know?

They say my lip gloss is poppin'; my lip gloss is cool.

All the boys keep jockin', they chase me after school.

VERSE 1

Mac L'Oreal, yep, 'cause I'm worth it. Love the way I puts it on so perfect.

Wipe the corners of my mouth so I work it. When I walk down the hallway, they can't say nothin'.

Oh, oh, oh, my lips so luscious, the way I spice it up with the Mac-Mac brushes.

L'Oreal got them wat-ballermelon crushes. That's probably the reason all these boys got crushes.

REPEAT CHORUS

VERSE 2
When it's time for lunch, my lips still rock. Lil Mama melon with the hot pink top.

Cherry, vanilla, flavors is a virtue. They lovin', lip gloss universal.

The boys really like it, the girls don't speak; rollin' they eyes, they lip gloss cheap.

It ain't my fault, but I could upgrade ya. Show you how to use nice things with nice flavors.

REPEAT CHORUS

BRIDGE 1
'Cause my lip gloss is poppin', is poppin', is poppin', is poppin'.

'Cause my lip gloss is poppin', is poppin', is poppin', is poppin'.

VERSE 3
Sittin' in eighth period, thought I was in trouble.

Dean called me on the loudspeaker on the double.

I stepped in her office like, "Yes, Ms. McClarkson?"

She like, "Girl, ran out of my lip gloss and write down where you get yours from,

'Cause I must admit, that bubblegum is poppin', is poppin', is poppin'." She ain't frontin'.

BRIDGE 2
And, uh, I be lovin' it, I be, I be lovin' it, uh.

I be usin' it, I be, I be usin' it, uh.

I be rubbin' it, I be, I be rubbin' it.

On my lips, my lips, my lip gloss.

REPEAT CHORUS

Words and Music by W. James Chambers II and Niatia Jessica Kirkland

DYNAMITE

BTS

Key of Recording: E (F# after the key change)
Key of Notation: G
Form of Recording: Intro–Verse 1–Pre-Chorus–Chorus–Verse 2–Pre-Chorus–Chorus–Bridge–Interlude–Chorus–(Key Change)
(For Use with Section 11 of the *Modern Band Bass Method*)

Song Tips:

- The original recording of this song has a key change before the last chorus. This concept is not covered in the Modern Band Methods. If you would like to add this to your performance, talk to your teacher about it, as it would require you and your bandmates to learn several new notes and chords.
- Though the timing of the chord changes is different in the verse and chorus, the chord progression doesn't change. Be sure to practice switching between these two progressions until you feel comfortable playing both.
- In the verses, the bass line of this song focuses on playing on the *downbeat* (beat 1) of each measure. Leading back to beat 1, the bass also plays a few ornamental notes and passing tones. Explore different notes here to discover what sounds good in these elaborations. Also, listen closely to the original recording to hear how the bassist combines long and short notes to enhance the rhythm of the bass line.

Intro/Chorus/Bridge/Interlude:

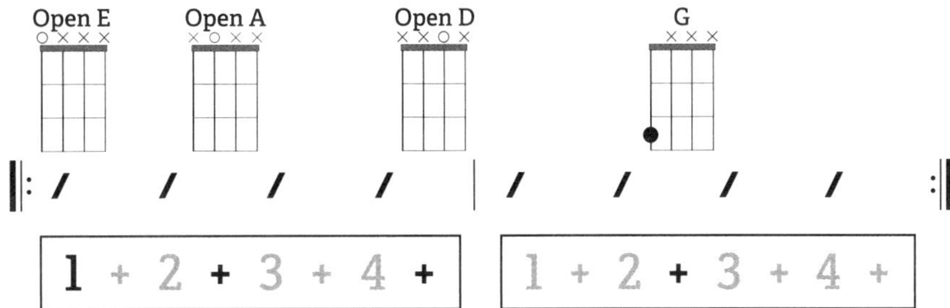

Verse/Pre-Chorus:

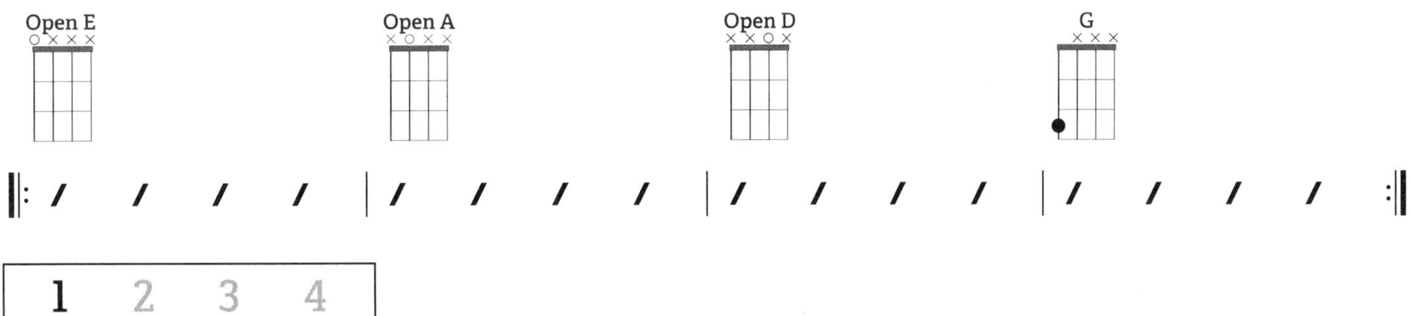

G Major Pentatonic Scale:

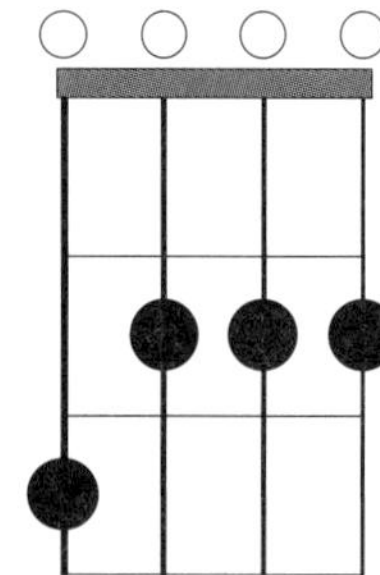

INTRO

Emi Ami D G
'Cause, ah-ah, I'm in the stars tonight.

Emi Ami D G
So watch me bring the fire and set the night alight.

VERSE 1

Emi Ami
Shoes on, get up in the morn', cup of milk, let's rock and roll.

D G
King Kong, kick the drum, rolling on like a rolling stone.

Emi Ami
Sing song when I'm walking home, jump up to the top, LeBron.

D G
Ding-dong, call me on my phone, iced tea, and a game of ping-pong.

PRE-CHORUS

Emi Ami
This is getting heavy. Can you hear the bass boom? I'm ready.

D G
Life is sweet as honey. Yeah, this beat cha-ching like money.

Emi Ami
Disco overload, I'm into that, I'm good to go.

D G
I'm diamond, you know I glow up. Hey, so let's go.

CHORUS

Emi Ami D G
'Cause, ah-ah, I'm in the stars tonight.

Emi Ami D G
So watch me bring the fire and set the night alight.

Emi Ami D G
Shining through the city with a little funk and soul.

Emi Ami D G
So I'm-a light it up like dynamite, whoa.

VERSE 2

Emi **Ami**
Bring a friend, join the crowd, whoever wanna come along.

D **G**
Word up, talk the talk, just move like we off the wall.

Emi **Ami**
Day or night, the sky's alight, so we dance to the break of dawn.

D **G**
Ladies and gentlemen, I got the medicine so you should keep ya eyes on the ball, huh.

REPEAT PRE-CHORUS

REPEAT CHORUS

BRIDGE

Emi **Ami** **D** **G**
Dy-na-na-na, na-na, na-na, na, na-na-na, life is dynamite.

Emi **Ami** **D** **G**
Dy-na-na-na, na-na, na-na, na, na-na-na, life is dynamite.

Emi **Ami** **D** **G**
Shining through the city with a little funk and soul.

Emi **Ami** **D** **G**
So I'm-a light it up like dynamite, whoa.

INTERLUDE

Emi **Ami** **D** **G**
Dy-na-na-na, na-na, na-na, ay. Dy-na-na-na, na-na, na-na, ay.

Emi **Ami** **D** **G**
Dy-na-na-na, na-na, na-na, ay. Light it up like dynamite.

Emi **Ami** **D** **G**
Dy-na-na-na, na-na, na-na, ay. Dy-na-na-na, na-na, na-na, ay.

Emi **Ami** **D** **G**
Dy-na-na-na, na-na, na-na, ay. Light it up like dynamite.

REPEAT CHORUS

GOODBYE LOOKS GOOD ON YOU

Alana Springsteen ft. Mitchell Tenpenny

Key of Recording: E
Key of Notation: G
Form of Recording: Intro–Verse 1–Pre-Chorus 1–Chorus–Verse 2–Pre-Chorus 2–Chorus–Interlude–Pre-Chorus 3–Chorus–Outro
(For Use with Section 11 of the *Modern Band Bass Method*)

Song Tips:

- In this arrangement, the guitars switch between playing muted power chords for the verses and big open chords for the pre-choruses and choruses. A simple yet effective way to support this as a bassist is to play the root notes of the power chords using shorter note lengths and long, sustained tones for the "bigger" pre-chorus and chorus sections.
- Try adding some octave notes to your bass line for this song. Experiment by adding octaves in different parts of the song and use your ears to decide what sounds best.

Intro/Verse/Interlude/Outro:

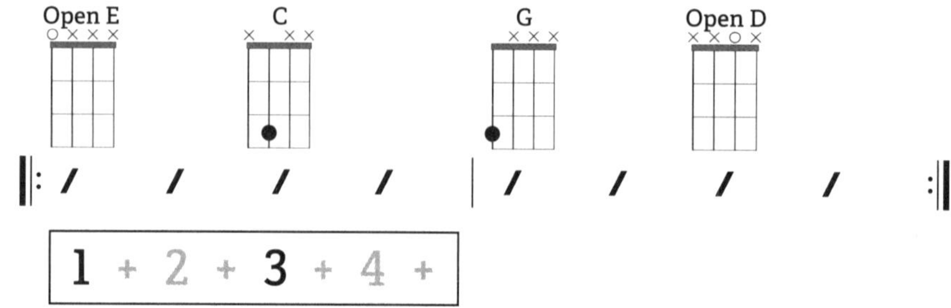

Pre-Chorus:

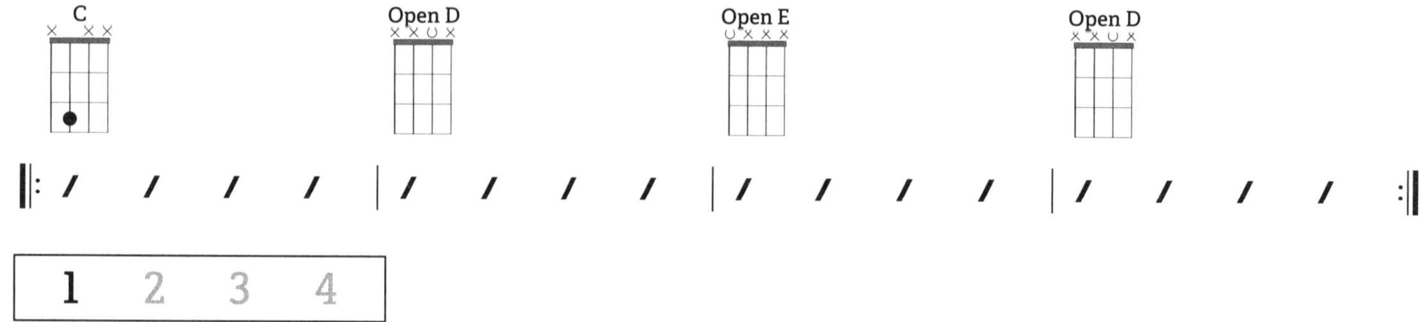

Chorus:

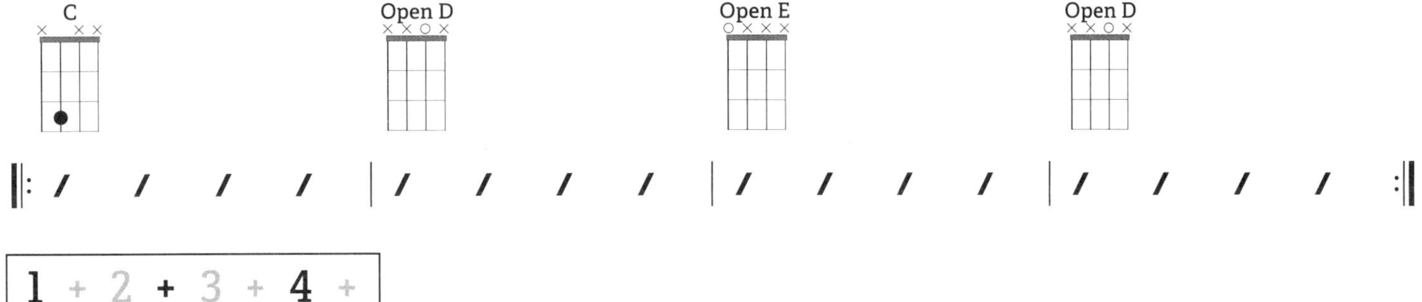

G Major Pentatonic Scale:

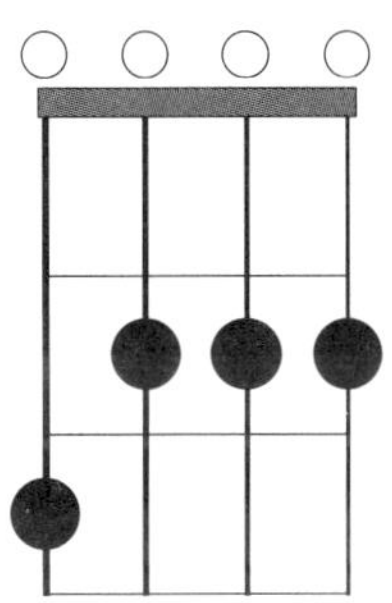

VERSE 1

Emi **C** **G** **D**
I know the rules of a break-up, delete your number and ruin your name.

Emi **C** **G** **D**
Baby, we can make a mess and make up, lie about it if I stay at your place.

PRE-CHORUS 1

C **D**
We could both be angry; hate you and you hate me.

Emi **D**
We can play that game and stay the same.

CHORUS

C **D**
But what if we don't have to choose? What if no one has to lose?

Emi **D**
I hope you meet somebody who loves you like I couldn't do.

C **D**
'Cause baby, you and me were never right, but we ain't gotta be on different sides.

Emi **D**
So what if we just told the truth, yeah, goodbye looks good on you, and it looks good on me

VERSE 2

Emi **C** **G** **D**
Too, ooh-ooh, ooh-ooh.

Emi **C** **G** **D**
We ain't gotta make a heartbreak harder. You ain't gotta make your mama hate me.

Emi **C** **G** **D**
I ain't gotta be a midtown martyr. I don't need a new girl to save me.

PRE-CHORUS 2

C **D**
We can still have the same friends, the same friends. We can sit at the same bar,

Emi **D**
Yeah, at the same bar. I just want you happy and hope you are.

REPEAT CHORUS

PRE-CHORUS 3

C **D**
We could both be angry; hate you and you hate me.

Emi **D**
We can play that game, but not today.

REPEAT CHORUS

HIGH HOPES

Panic! At the Disco

Key of Recording: F
Key of Notation: F
Form of Recording: Intro–Verse 1–Pre-Chorus 1–Chorus–Verse 2–Pre-Chorus 2–Chorus
(For Use with Section 12 of the *Modern Band Bass Method*)

Song Tips:

- The verse and chorus of this song have the same chord progression, but each has its own feel. The verse is calmer, while the chorus is louder and has more energy. To practice this contrast, rehearse playing the same chord progression with both high energy and low energy. This could mean playing with different dynamics, different comping patterns, or different instrumentation among your bandmates. Experiment by playing with more or less energy with your bandmates.
- The bassist for the studio recording and live performances of this song uses a 5-string bass, so some of the bass notes are lower than what can be played on a standard 4-string bass. The rhythmic patterns of the bass, like those of most of the instruments in this song, change regularly. Bass players should ensure they are in sync with one another to match the rhythms they are playing. This may involve using the exact comping patterns indicated in this book, or listening to recordings or live performances for inspiration on how to add variety. The bass serves as both a rhythmic instrument and a pitched one, so the way bassists play can significantly influence the overall feel of the music. Utilize this concept to introduce variety in different sections of the song.

Intro:

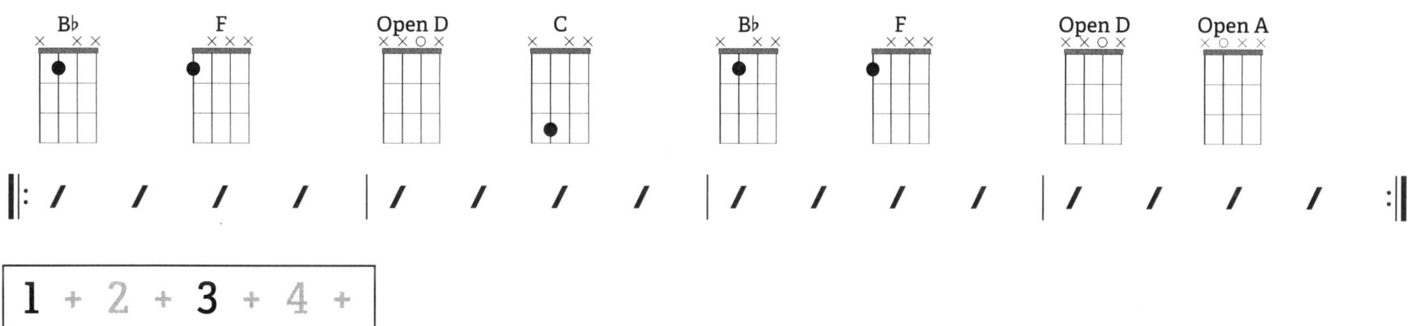

Verse/Chorus:

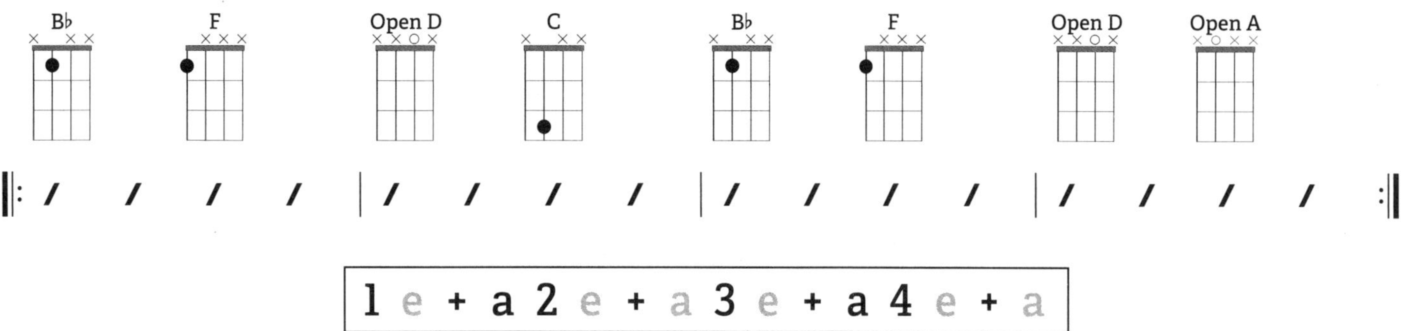

Pre-Chorus:

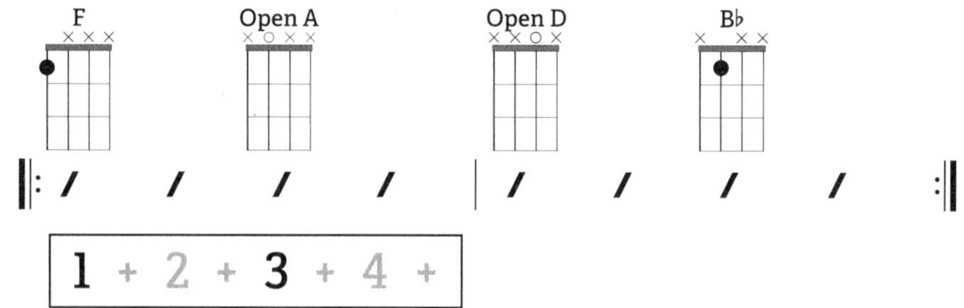

F Major Pentatonic Scale:

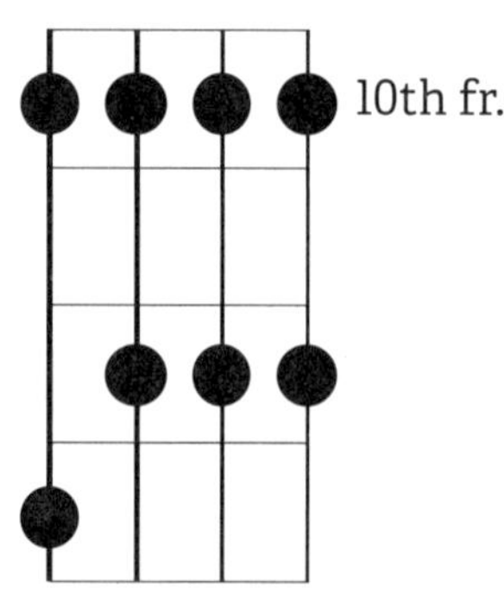

INTRO

B♭ F Dmi C
Had to have high, high hopes for a living. Shooting for the stars when I couldn't make a killing.

B♭ F Dmi Ami
Didn't have a dime, but I always had a vision. Always had high, high hopes.

B♭ F Dmi C
Had to have high, high hopes for a living. Didn't know how, but I always had a feeling.

B♭ F Dmi Ami
I was gonna be that one in a million. Always had high, high hopes.

VERSE 1

B♭ F Dmi C
Mama said, "Fulfill the prophecy. Be something greater, go make a legacy."

B♭ F Dmi Ami
Manifest destiny, back in the days we wanted everything, wanted everything.

B♭ F Dmi C
Mama said, "Burn your biographies. Rewrite your history, light up your wildest dreams."

B♭ F Dmi Ami
Museum victories every day. We wanted everything, wanted everything.

PRE-CHORUS 1

F A Dmi B♭mi
Mama said, "Don't give up, it's a little complicated.

F A Dmi B♭mi
All tied up, no more love and I'd hate to see you waiting."

CHORUS

B♭ F Dmi C
Had to have high, high hopes for a living. Shooting for the stars when I couldn't make a killing.

B♭ F Dmi Ami
Didn't have a dime but I always had a vision. Always had high, high hopes.

B♭ F Dmi C
Had to have high, high hopes for a living. Didn't know how, but I always had a feeling.

B♭ F Dmi Ami
I was gonna be that one in a million. Always had high, high hopes.

VERSE 2

B♭ F Dmi C
Mama said, "It's uphill for oddities. Stranger crusaders ain't ever wannabes."

B♭ F Dmi Ami
The weird and the novelties that don't ever change. We wanted everything, wanted everything.

B♭ F Dmi C
Stay up on that rise. Stay up on that rise and never come down, oh.

B♭ F Dmi Ami
Stay up on that rise. Stay up on that rise and never come down.

PRE-CHORUS 2

F A Dmi B♭mi
Mama said, "Don't give up, it's a little complicated.

F A Dmi B♭mi
All tied up, no more love and I'd hate to see you waiting."

F A Dmi B♭mi
They say it's all been done, but they haven't seen the best of me-eh-eh-eh.

F A Dmi B♭mi
So I got one more run and it's gonna be a sight to see-eh-eh-eh.

REPEAT CHORUS (2 TIMES)

CAN'T REMEMBER TO FORGET YOU

Shakira ft. Rihanna

Key of Recording: B Minor
Key of Notation: B Minor
Form of Recording: Intro–Verse 1–Chorus 1–Interlude–Verse 2–Chorus 1–Bridge–Chorus 2
(For Use with Section 12 of the *Modern Band Bass Method*)

Song Tips:

- A key feature of this song is the stylistic difference between the groovy verse and the heavier rock chorus. There are a few key elements that help create this difference in sound. As the bass player, you can help define the contrast by listening closely to the original bass player's approach. Pay attention to the length of each note and always strive for reliable timing and attack.
- The recorded bass line for this song is quite busy, fast, and syncopated. Students can use the staff and tab notation to learn the bass line as recorded, or they can use the chords as a reference and create their own pattern.

Intro/Verse/Pre-Chorus:

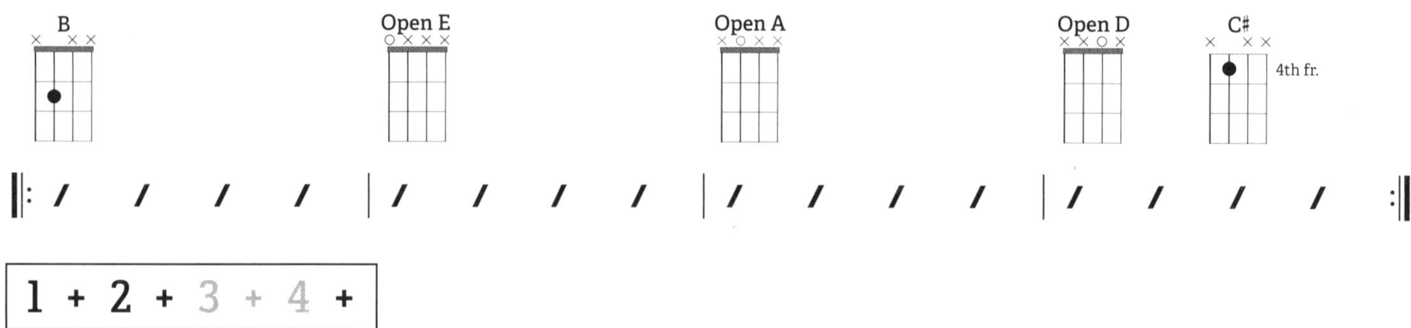

Chorus:

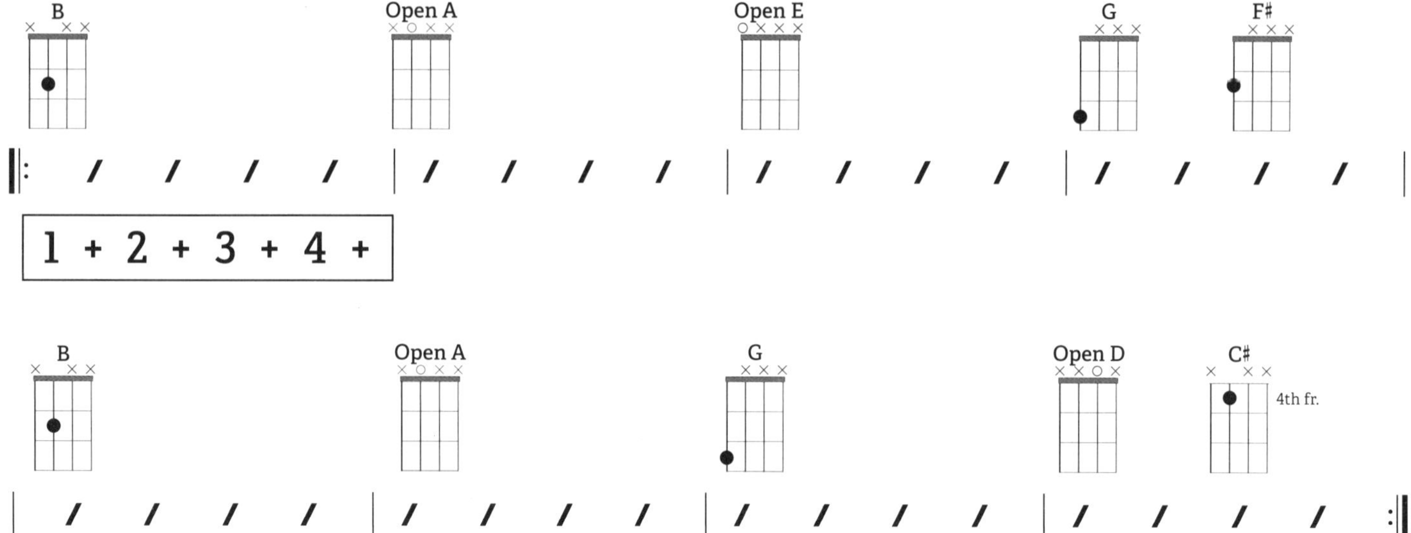

Bass Tab (Verse):

Bass Tab (Chorus):

B Minor Pentatonic Scale:

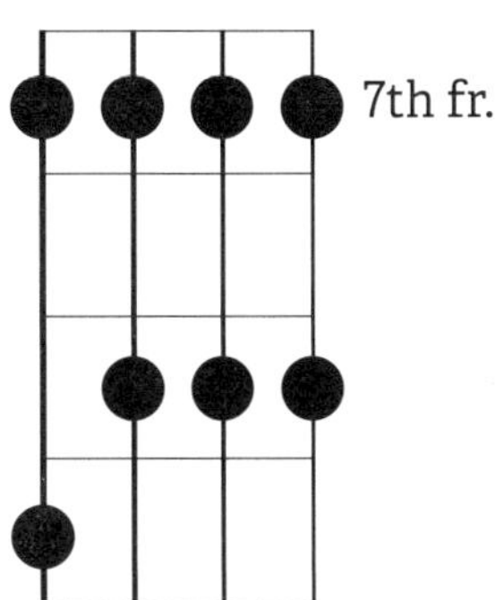

VERSE 1

Bmi   Emi   A   D
I left a note on my bedpost saying not to repeat yesterday's mistakes.

Bmi   Emi   A   D
What I tend to do when it comes to you, I see only the good, selective memory.

Bmi   Emi   A   D
The way you make me feel, yeah, you gotta hold on me. I've never met someone so different.

           Bmi   Emi   A
Oh, here we go, you're part of me now, you're part of me. So where you go, I follow, follow, follow.

CHORUS 1

Bmi   A   Emi   G   F♯mi
Oh-oh-oh-oh, oh. Oh-oh-oh-oh, oh. I can't remember to forget you.

Bmi   A   G   D   C♯mi
Oh-oh-oh-oh, oh. Oh-oh-oh-oh, oh. I keep forgetting I should let you

Bmi   A   Emi   G   F♯mi
Go. But when you look at me, the only memory is us kissing in the moonlight.

Bmi   A   G
Oh-oh-oh-oh, oh. Oh-oh-oh-oh, oh. I can't remember to forget you.

INTERLUDE

Bmi Emi   A   D
Ooh, ooh, oh-oh, oh. I can't remember to forget you.

Bmi Emi   A   D
Ooh, ooh, oh-oh, oh.

VERSE 2

Bmi   Emi   A   D
I go back again, fall off the train, land in his bed, repeat yesterday's mistakes.

Bmi   Emi   A   D
What I'm tryin' to say is not to forget. You see only the good, selective memory.

Bmi   Emi   A   D
The way he makes me feel like, the way he makes me feel, I never seemed to act so stupid.

           Bmi   Emi   A
Oh, here we go, he a part of me now, he a part of me. So where he goes, I follow, follow, follow.

REPEAT CHORUS 1

BRIDGE

Bmi Emi A D
I rob and I kill to keep him with me. I'll do anything for that boy.

Bmi Emi A D
I'd give my last dime to hold him tonight. I'll do anything for that boy.

Bmi Emi A D
I rob and I kill to keep him with me. I'll do anything for that boy.

Bmi Emi A D
I'd give my last dime to hold him tonight. I'll do anything for that boy.

CHORUS 2

Bmi A Emi G F♯mi
Oh-oh-oh-oh, oh. Oh-oh-oh-oh, oh. I can't remember to forget you.

Bmi A G D C♯mi
Oh-oh-oh-oh, oh. Oh-oh-oh-oh, oh. I keep forgetting I should let you

Bmi A Emi G F♯mi
Go. But when you look at me, the only memory is us kissing in the moonlight.

Bmi A Emi G F♯mi
Oh-oh-oh-oh, oh. Oh-oh-oh-oh, oh. I can't remember to forget you.

Bmi A Emi G F♯mi
But when you look at me, the only memory is us kissing in the moonlight.

Bmi A G
Oh-oh-oh-oh, oh. Oh-oh-oh-oh, oh. I can't remember to forget you.